KU-755-753

HOLY INNOCENTS:
GRIEVING FOR THE DEATH OF A BABY

MARGARET SPARSHOTT

HOLY INNOCENTS:
GRIEVING FOR THE DEATH OF A BABY

AUSTIN & MACAULEY

Copyright © Margaret Sparshott
Illustrated with pencil drawings by the author.

All names within this book have been changed to protect the identities of those involved, unless otherwise stated

The right of Margaret Sparshott to be identified as author of this work has been asserted by her in accordance with section 77 and 78 of the Copyright, Designs and Patents Act 1988.

All rights reserved. No part of this publication may be reproduced, stored in a retrieval system, or transmitted in any form or by any means, electronic, mechanical, photocopying, recording, or otherwise, without the prior permission of the publishers.

Any person who commits any unauthorized act in relation to this publication may be liable to criminal prosecution and civil claims for damages.

I am grateful to, and have great admiration for, the people whose personal experiences are quoted in the book. To respect their privacy their names have been changed, except for those whose stories have been referenced.

A CIP catalogue record for this title is
available from the British Library.

ISBN 978 1 905609 49 9

www.austinmacauley.com

First Published (2009)
Austin & Macauley Publishers Ltd.
25 Canada Square
Canary Wharf
London
E14 5LB

Printed & Bound in Great Britain

DEDICATION

For Sarah and Jeremy.

Dedicated to those who have lived through the pain

This book is full of stories of people who have survived the pain of losing a loved and wanted child. Pain is not good but it can be withstood; the goodness and greatness are in the people, living, working and loving through so much pain.

If you take up the book and read to the end, then perhaps you will see that, underneath the pain, there can be a spring-like flowering.

ACKNOWLEDGEMENTS

My grateful thanks to Joan Copeland and Pauline Cornish for reading the book in its early stages and helping me to see my way more clearly; and to Gay Jarman for checking the proofs. My thanks also to the many friends and professional colleagues who have shared their experiences with me; and especially to my sister Elizabeth, for her support and encouragement in all my work, throughout my life.

Among the many others who have given me their support, I am indebted to the Rt. Revd. Christopher Budd, Roman Catholic Bishop of Plymouth, for listening to me and for lending me books; to Father Gregory Carpenter of the Orthodox Church in Plymouth; to the Chief Rabbi's office; to the IQRA Trust for their Science Work Card Series; and to the paediatric anaesthetist K.J.S. Anand, member of the International Association of the Study of Pain and responsible himself for the relief of much suffering, for sharing his vision of the destiny of the soul in the Sikh religion, which moved me very much. My thanks also to Jenni Thomas OBE for writing the Forward to this book; I have learned much from her through the Child Bereavement Charity.

I also owe an immense debt of gratitude to the late Lady Lothian OBE for the interest and support she has shown in my work. She has done so much to improve the lives of preborn and newborn babies through her work for the National Council of Women, and as Chairman of the Trustees of the Women and Children's Welfare Fund. She is sadly missed.

THE DEATH STELE:

Amphorete with her grand-daughter, reproduced with kind permission from the director of the Kerameikos Museum, Athens

Here I hold my daughter's dead child. I used to hold her in my lap, when in life our eyes beheld the sun's rays. Now we are both dead, I hold her still.

.

All names within this book have been changed to protect the identities of those involved, unless otherwise stated.

CONTENTS

FOREWORD
By Jenni Thomas O.B.E.

I am delighted to write the foreword for this book, which so movingly explains how parents feel when they experience the death of their baby.

This book focuses on an aspect of loss that is often neglected and not seen as a significant loss – pregnancy loss and the death of a baby. 'Holy Innocents' should help not only parents who have experienced the death of a baby but will also provide an invaluable insight into this type of loss for professionals. A particularly powerful aspect of this book is the first-hand accounts from parents.

The importance of recognising their varied needs is a theme that I so welcome in each of the chapters of this book; we can only begin our search for the understanding of what a baby's death means to parents if those in the professional field can listen and listen carefully to what grieving families say they experience.

As this book illustrates so clearly there is a connectedness between parent and child, an attachment that begins long before birth. The author highlights the value of respecting each situation as individual and also writes that not only are the family members individual, but importantly that each baby is an individual.

Like the author, my background has been in the NHS where in the early 60's my interest in the emotional care of families began as a nursery nurse on a Special Care Baby Unit in Buckinghamshire. I was fortunate to work in an environment where parents were encouraged to stay with their baby and to have control in what they wanted for their child before, at and after death.

We as carers learnt from these parents much of what the author writes about in these pages. There is no relationship like that of parent and child; it is special despite the length of the pregnancy or life of the baby. Sadly, a baby's death at or soon after birth is often not acknowledged in society as being as meaningful as if the child had lived and made more contribution to the family.

Grieving means feeling all the sadness and the sorrow, all the anger, guilt and pain that loss can bring, and it also means doing something with those feelings. This book is about what it feels like to grieve. It is also about expressing grief. Many of the feelings that are described are feelings that people grieving for all kinds of different reasons will recognise. But this book is about one particular experience of grief – the grief that follows the loss of a baby.

Grieving is never easy, but grieving for a baby can be especially hard. The death of a baby is so shocking. It's a death that should never happen. There seems no reason why a baby should die and for many parents, no reason is discovered for their baby's death. As a result, parents often blame themselves. They feel they have failed their baby and failed as parents. They feel angry with themselves, with doctors and nurses, with God. They feel bitter, because others have children and they have not. Above all, they feel desolation and despair because the baby they wanted has died, because their future together has been denied them, and because their love for their child has now no course to run.

Parents talk about the relief they feel when they hear other parents' stories and realise that they are neither alone nor abnormal. Reading other stories also puts them in touch with their own memories and feelings, and although this hurts, many say that the pain and tears are helpful.

'Holy Innocents' will speak to many families who are searching for meaning after the death of their child. Special attention is paid to the beliefs of major religions and how they view the spirituality and death of a baby.

Parents and families have to find their own ways of grieving. What is helpful for one parent may not be at all helpful for someone else. Each family is unique and we learn in the book from families who have other children recognising the needs these children have for honest explanation and understanding.

My learning has been continuous and new both as a professional and more recently as a bereaved grandmother myself. Despite all my experience, nothing could have prepared me for the call that came from my youngest son telling me that he and his wife were on their way to hospital – the hospital I am based in. His wife was in premature labour at just under 24 weeks, and they asked me to be with them. Walking into that hospital, where I had so many times before been part of the team supporting bereaved families, felt so different when it was my little grandchild who was being born just too early. All the things I'd learnt that were important to other families suddenly became hugely significant in this, our family crisis.

Annabelle was born alive a few hours later and lived for just a short while. As a mother, I felt overwhelming sadness for my son and truly lovely daughter-in-law; as a granny, I felt huge sadness for all Annabelle would not experience in life. I just wanted to pick her up and take her home, pretend everything was going to be all right. I would have done anything in my power to make things better, but the many hundreds of families I have seen over the years have taught me that this just can't be – there is no making it better. But three years on, much of the pain has lessened and the birth of a little grandson Dominic at 26 weeks – who thankfully survived – has helped to keep us all occupied and moving forward, never forgetting Annabelle who will always be my 6th grandchild. I feel immensely privileged to have been included in her short life and to have written about this in 'Farewell, my child'.

I am sure this book will help in lessening the isolation bereaved parents so often feel.

Jenni Thomas OBE,
Founder & President,
Child Bereavement Charity

INTRODUCTION

Nobody lives forever. At some time or another – early or late – each one of us must die. This means that we all of us must grieve for lost loved ones; grief then is part of life and has to be borne and surmounted. There are different strategies for doing this, varying in vocabulary and structure, but all with the same principle – that grieving is a process which needs to be completed before the mourner can absorb the grief and continue day to day life, with hopes as well as fears. This is what time should concede following the death of a parent, a partner, or a dear friend.

But what happens if the one who dies seems never to have lived at all? What happens if death occurs before the first breath is taken, or even before birth? The death of a baby or a very young child appears an unnatural death. The parents cannot mourn a life that is over, but they grieve for a life that has never begun. They do not mourn for a shared past, but for a future that will never be, with someone they have never known. These feelings are complicated by guilt and perplexity – guilt for their failure to produce a healthy child, perplexity that they cannot identify with what, or for whom, they are mourning.

On occasion society will make them feel that they should not be grieving at all, either by totally ignoring the loss, or by misplaced attempts at comfort. Very often parents are driven by mixed feelings to enter much too soon into another pregnancy, not giving themselves enough time to resolve their feelings for the last one, and unresolved grief leaves a lifelong wound. A substitute child can never replace one that is lost – indeed, should not be asked to do so.

Sometimes, too, the surviving children can suffer from the refusal of the parents to relinquish the dead child. The children may grieve, but their grief is contaminated by jealousy of the one who seems to block all their attempts to be needed for themselves. Because of these things, and for many other reasons, it is important for parents to recognise the 'identity' of the dead child, that is to say, who the child is, what has happened to him or her, and where he or she is to be found. They need to understand the relevance of the child to their lives before they can move on.

During a professional life spent for the most part caring for very sick or premature babies, I have often noticed that the parents of babies who die when or before they are born are deeply distressed, not only for the death of a long awaited child, but also by a great sense of futility. It seems as though the child has never existed.

This book is intended to show that babies who die have indeed existed, and that they may be mourned as the individual persons they were intended to be. To do this we must discuss the development of the fetus; whether preborn and newborn humans have personality, and if so, when and how it develops. Newborn babies cannot speak, but they have their own language in the way they behave, and this language can be read and understood by caregivers, whether they are professional or parental. By learning to read their baby's signals, parents of the very sick baby in hospital can take some control. The world of neonatal intensive care is a brutal one; even so, some comfort can be offered there, and as well as the end of life I shall also discuss the care of those babies who will survive the ordeal of intensive care, even if not for a very long time.

The part parents play in the drama of prenatal and neonatal illness and death is a vital one; even now their wishes and feelings are not always considered. But newborn babies, who may live or die, are not parcels damaged or lost in the post, to be apologised for, and for whom compensation is the end of the

24

mishap. Babies are persons, created by their parents, who deserve to be part of a family. To lose such a person is a tragedy, sometimes even described by mothers as a mutilation. But there is no disgrace in death; if death is to happen, at least it should be possible to avoid the pain and bitterness left when friends, relations and professional carers are thoughtless and unfeeling, sending the wrong signals. I hope to show in this book how the lives of babies, parents and professionals in hospital and in the community can bring mutual understanding and empathy, that some good feelings may mitigate the sorrow and regret.

Parents are not the only people to mourn lost babies; other members of the family, siblings and grandparents, professional carers also, each from their own point of view and in their own way, will suffer and need comfort. They too need help to resolve their bewilderment and distress.

Some parents rail against a God who allows babies to die even before they have had a chance to live a little. The God in whom they believed surely does not wish his children to suffer. Why, then, this pain, surely unmerited?

If there is such a thing as a soul, what is it? Can babies be said to have souls, since they have no sense of right or wrong? If they do have souls, what is the destination of this innocent soul when the baby dies, since some religious denominations would have us believe that all must perish due to original sin? What do the different world religions and creeds have to say about the early death of children? All this and more will be discussed in this book.

All professional people who care for babies in hospital and in the community, together with friends and relatives of the bereaved, have an important part to play in helping parents to understand they can grieve for their lost children as persons to be loved, and can rest in the knowledge that their short lives have not been an empty space. They may not have lived long, but their existence was real, continues to be real, and they can be mourned as real people, individual, irreplaceable, and innocent.

Author's note:

The baby in the womb, as well as the newborn baby, has a gender, so it is inappropriate always to refer to him/her as 'it'. In order to maintain simplicity, and to avoid having constantly to refer to the above 'him/her,' I will be using alternate chapters for boys and girls.

PART I
LIFE BEFORE BIRTH

The Unborn Daughter

On her unborn in the vast circle
Concentric with our finite lives
On her unborn, her name uncurling
Like a young fern within the mind;
On her unclothed with flesh or beauty
In the womb's darkness, I bestow
The formal influence of the will,
The wayward influence of the heart,
Weaving upon her fluid bones
The subtle fabric of her being,
Hair, hands and eyes, the body's texture,
Shot with the glory of the soul.

R.S.Thomas

CHAPTER ONE
WHAT IS A BABY?

'Good women, I have for your good and not for my own, traced the beginnings of myself and you from the tools whereby we were made, and the manner we were made of, to what we were, when we were but an embryo.'

From: Culpepper's Book of Birth (1985)

The newborn baby has been described as *'a biological system of uncontrolled apertures'* by Eric Linklater, and *'a loud noise at one end and no sense of responsibility at the other'* by Ogden Nash – but is that really all a baby is? Some mothers, tired after a day washing, drying, feeding and comforting a fractious child, would say 'yes!' But there will be times when all mothers, watching over a placidly sleeping baby, or meeting the suddenly intense scrutiny of the infant waking up to the world, would say 'No! There is more to my baby than loud noises and uncontrolled apertures!' What more, then, is there to a baby?

Babies are much more than helpless objects that need to be changed and fed. Even at six months gestational age, the preterm baby shows preferences and characteristics, as well as great fortitude, even if lacking in strength. Observing them as they struggle against a hostile environment which they are not yet formed to inhabit, they can be seen to wake up to the world, begin to look about them, begin to complain, demand, show signs of satisfaction, obstinately insist they want to live. These things cannot be shown by speech because babies cannot speak for themselves, but they have ways of making their feelings felt; for instance, the helpless objects that need to be changed and fed can make a loud noise when they feel it is time for this to happen. Their lack of words, however, means that they depend on others to translate their behaviour, so they have advocates and prosecutors who speak for and against them, depending on personal agenda. My agenda is to speak in favour of babies, whom I see as persons in the making, and it is from this position I write this book.

Words and their misuse

Newspaper pictures of the 21-week-old preborn baby grasping the surgeon's finger through the incision while undergoing surgery in the womb show an event that seems miraculous, but what you have seen you may believe – babies of this gestational age can do this. But if the headline had mentioned the word 'fetus', would the reaction of many people have been one of repugnance? The truth is that words can conjure up an image that has little to do with their meaning, and those who want to influence how people think have used this fact. What is it in words that can elicit disgust and eliminate sympathy?

One medical dictionary defines the fetus, or embryo, as: *'the name given to the child while still within the womb'* – so already a potential child. Unfortunately, for many people, the word 'fetus' has lost this innocent meaning, and the fetus is visualised as something ugly, ill-formed, lying in a sink in a muddle of blood products. A young woman on a radio programme once described one of two lovers as disgusting, *'like a fetus'*, because of her ugliness; such a creature (it was suggested) should never show love in public. Sadly, this remark was greeted with laughter. But is it only the beautiful that can be loved? Many of us would not fare well if that is the case!

For those of us involved in the care of very premature babies, 'fetus' does not conjure up a vision of ugliness or unnaturalness; a fetus is not a waste product. Nor is it so for the happily pregnant mother; for her, the fetus is her unborn child, who will be mourned if he is born before time. Indeed many photographers have shown the fetus in its beauty of potential growth. There for our wonder and delight is the newspaper picture of the fetus clutching the surgeon's hand as he operates through the open uterus; there is the fetus sucking his thumb; the fetus cradled in his primordial fluid, dreaming to awaken. These images of the fetus are not repulsive but of a rare beauty, strange only because the unborn baby has not hitherto been seen.

The word 'preborn' is not in the dictionary, but it is used by many, including some of the medical profession, who, when talking to prospective parents, are attempting to avoid the ugly images conjured up by 'fetus'. It describes the human infant in the process of formation before birth – but both 'fetus' and 'preborn' describe the same creature, no existent or invented words can change that. It is important that people, not just medical professionals but men and women with their own special place in the community, understand that there is no difference between the fetus and the preborn. It is saddening that words can be used to suggest ugliness and disgust where there is only a miracle of complexity and potential.

None the less, terms used are important; when speaking to parents the words we use matter. Women who lose their babies before birth do not like to hear them described as 'fetuses', even if this is the correct medical term. These mothers are struggling to come to terms with the loss of a baby, and it will not be helpful to pretend that what they lost was not a 'baby', as we shall see later on.

What is an embryo?

Originally, the embryo was considered to be the developing human being from conception to six weeks' gestation. More recently it has been suggested that the term 'pre-embryo' would be a better definition for the fertilised egg up to the implantation stage, which is usually completed at about fourteen days with the appearance of the **primitive streak** (a series of cells at one end of the embryonic disc, which is considered to be the first recognisable feature of an embryo). This distinction has caused controversy amongst experts, as it questions the time at which an embryo becomes a human being (in other words, a person). Many experts continue to refer to the embryo as the 'post-conception' stage, as the cluster of cells which form this pre-embryo are simply non-differentiated cells with no specific function.

The words 'cluster of cells' can also be used by those promoting the use of embryonic stem cells in research for the treatment of genetic disorders. This cluster of cells is the **blastocyst** which will, when it reaches the implantation stage, have the potential to develop into a human baby – but the blastocyst is not itself a miniature baby; many thousands are lost quite naturally without anyone being the wiser.

The contemporary ethical problem is whether life should be created as a commodity; should the potential of these cells to develop guarantee them protection against deliberate destruction, no matter how advantageous this would be for those already alive? A blastocyst is a source of embryonic stem cells, a source of material which could be used for tissue repair, or for reversing degenerative diseases such as Huntington's chorea, cystic fibrosis, or sickle-cell anaemia; it would be most wonderful to be able to put a stop to the inheritance of such diseases. On the other hand, although the early embryo is not a human person, it has the potential to become one; is it right to use a potential human as a commodity? This is not just a case of Christian versus non-Christian; there are differing views amongst Christians and Humanists themselves. Basically, our religion, the worldview and our personal philosophy may affect our decision as to what is right or wrong.

What is a fetus?

At about fourteen days, a small mound of cells appears which forms a track down the centre of the embryo; this is the 'primitive streak', which is the genesis of the primordial nervous system. From then on, the embryo grows and develops with tremendous energy, and after eight weeks is sufficiently well developed to be called a fetus, which is the term used to describe the developing human being from six weeks gestation to the time of birth. The name means 'offspring', and this is the name by which it will be called until it is born.

During pregnancy the brain develops at a startling rate, as can be seen by the two drawings of the human brain at eight weeks gestation and at term. Babies are busy learning all the time, and sensory perception begins early in pregnancy. Tactile sensation, taste and smell develop in the early months, and hearing is fully functioning by 25 to 27 weeks' gestation. It is now well known that babies can hear and recognise the voices of their parents from within the womb, and also become accustomed to music that is frequently played. On the whole babies like soothing, rhythmical tunes, but they also tend to have the same tastes in music as their mothers, and can recognise signature tunes of favourite radio and television programmes. Vision achieves functional status only approaching the last trimester, and even then is poorly developed – but then babies have no need of vision before birth.

THE FOETAL BRAIN AT EIGHT WEEKS - sagittal section showings parts of the midbrain

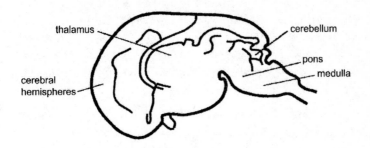

thalamus

cerebellum

pons

medulla

cerebral hemispheres

THE BRAIN OF A TERM INFANT AT BIRTH
the brain stem and the midbrain are more fully developed
than the cortex, which develops rapidly over the first few years

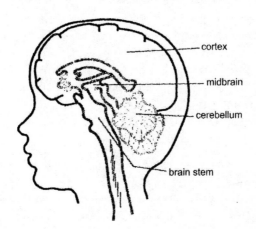

cortex

midbrain

cerebellum

brain stem

The baby as a person

What is the nature of humanity? Biological scientist John Bryant presents different perspectives. There is **Chemistry**: according to Joni Mitchell '*We are stardust/We are golden/We are billion year old carbon*'. There is **Biology**: '*we are mammals – we differ from mice in only a few hundred genes*', or: '*We are the most complex of living organisms, capable of self consciousness, rationality, intellect, language, moral reasoning …*' And there is **Spirituality**: '*We are made in the image of God.*'[1]

Charles le Gai Eaton, in his book 'Islam and the Destiny of Man' asks the question: '*For who is this person? Is he myself as a baby or as a child, as a youth caught in the net of joy, middle aged, senile at the moment of death? We cannot locate him with any certainty.*'[2]

If 'being a person' means being able to respond to one's surroundings, as some think, then at eight weeks the fetus is a person. However, there is a wide diversity in opinion as to when a baby becomes a person; so diverse that, according to Carmel Bagness in her book 'Genetics, the Fetus and our Future', '*it is questionable as to whether one answer is possible in such a pluralist society.*'[3] Some people believe being 'a person' means the ability to be self-aware: '*any being capable of valuing its own existence.*'[4] This definition would not only rule out personhood for newborn babies, but also for children suffering from severe learning disabilities, and even those who have lost their ability to reason through accident, illness or old age.

Some people believe that the fetus should be respected as a person from conception, even if only the potential is there and as yet no sensation or response has been detected. Others consider that a baby can only be considered a viable human being after birth, but preterm babies, even those born at 26 weeks' gestation, certainly show human characteristics, even signs of individuality. Preterm babies can show preferences for the position in which they lie, for instance, and will react strongly with grimaces and agitated body movements at things they dislike. On the other hand, a preterm baby can show by his relaxed and tucked position that he is comfortable and unstressed.

John V. Taylor, in his book 'The Go Between God', contrasts life before and after birth as: *'life in the womb is water-life in which the foetus can know neither separateness nor otherness. Afterwards we are born into air-life in which growth can only come through separateness.'* [5] Certainly the body at birth undergoes changes which appear miraculous, in that so rarely does anything go wrong. But in fact the baby is the same, an hour before and an hour after its passage from dark to light, only it is in a different element and a different place.

Whether or not they can be called persons, one thing is certain – babies have a truly amazing stamina! Preterm babies – even very tiny ones – will fight doggedly to live, even against the odds of gross immaturity, evidenced in the fragile skin, the inability to feed and the lungs that are not yet sufficiently formed to function properly. They inspire admiration and respect in their professional carers. When they survive and do well, we all rejoice; when the incompatibilities of the outside world are too much for them and they succumb, everybody grieves.

According to Carmel Bagness, the general consensus seems to be that, even as the exact moment of passage from youth to middle age cannot be identified, the progress to personhood cannot be given a beginning or an end but is an ongoing process. Most parents would certainly perceive their infants as being persons! A mother recognises the personality of her baby long before that baby is born. Fathers, too, can tell stories of the wonderful kicks they receive from their unborn children, conjuring up visions of future football stars!

The embryo, the preborn/fetus and the baby are all part of the progression to personhood; if they should die, it is to a person the parents say 'goodbye.'

Dreams and memories

There is evidence to show that babies dream in the womb. Nikki Bradford discusses dreams and memory in her book 'The Miraculous World of Your Unborn Baby', quoting Dr. Thomas Verny, who says: *'the first thin slivers of memory track begin streaking across the foetal brain'* [6] during the final three months of pregnancy. Rapid eye-movement-sleep (REM) which indicates dreaming can be detected at about 23 weeks gestation, which would give babies 17 weeks to dream in the womb before birth. What do they dream about? *'Things they find interesting enough to relive while asleep',* says Dr. Verny. *'The things they have been doing too – moving their feet and hands, playing with the umbilical cord, hearing sounds, and reliving any powerful emotions the mother may have experienced that day and of which they have also been aware.'* Dr. David Chamberlain, President of the Association for Pre- and Perinatal Psychology and Health, believes that unborn babies are *'processing their own thoughts, feelings and life experiences to date, much as the rest of us do in dreams.'* [7]

Memories of events in the womb, and of the actual birth, are well documented. A study by Dr. Chamberlain reported remarkably accurate birth memories, and several of these concerned feelings of being intelligent personalities. One young woman said: *'I felt I knew a lot … I never thought of being a person … I thought I was an intelligent mind.'* One such pre-birth memory came to light on a counselling course during a discussion on the relationship between experiences in infancy and stress in adulthood:

> Suddenly, Pat found herself describing a dream that had upset her very much at the time, but thought she had

forgotten. She was in a dark place, trying to climb up and out to the light by means of a strong cord, which she described as being 'like an umbilical cord.' But then it seemed she was climbing four cords in turn, each one more thin and frail than the one before. The last cord she had to climb was so fragile she knew that soon it would break. Beneath her, there was nothing but a dark void into which she was going to fall; looking up, she saw above her a woman's face – a young woman, dark, with short straight hair. As she watched, the woman turned her face away, ignoring not only the danger Pat was in but also her mere presence. 'It was my mother; I found out later she had diphtheria during her pregnancy and was very ill – she nearly died and so did I. Her illness terrified and exhausted her; I was an impediment that stole her energy, and she failed to bond – and after that, she always seemed distant to me.'

As she told this dream half a lifetime later, Pat became so distressed the group had to support her physically. Pat firmly believes that the dream was in fact a memory of the horrible danger she was in before she was born, when she became aware of the threat of death, and the death of love.

Mothers and babies

The relationship between each mother and baby is unique. To the consciousness of every mother her child is an individual who yet belongs to her own destiny. In her experience of this primal relationship, every mother is **the** mother, every child is **the** child, and the relationship between them is **the** primal relationship.

At one time newborn babies were thought of as 'clean slates', as they could have no past experience, traditional values or social consciousness to influence their behaviour. They were considered passive receptacles of outside experience, incapable of reaction and without control over themselves or their environment. All the baby had to do was grow; all he needed for this purpose was a source of food, and a shield against the outside world; all these things his mother could provide. At this stage, then, there was considered to be no real sense of 'self', but in retrospect it seems that even the fetus may have some comprehension of the uterine environment, as learning begins.

If something occurs during pregnancy to upset this nourishing and accepting relationship, the baby will no longer be able to thrive, and this upset can be related to maternal stress, as well as physiological factors such as infection, malnutrition, and alcohol and drug abuse. Pre-birth experience, even if it can only be recalled in dream-like fashion, is of crucial importance to the growing individual.

In his book 'The Child', the psychotherapist Erich Neumann, a pupil of Carl Jung, describes the special relationship between mothers and their babies as *'participation mystique'*, [8] meaning a subconscious, non-verbal understanding – both are sensitive to the feelings and needs of the other. If she is ill, unhappy or stressed, her feelings are transmitted to her growing child and will inhibit the rate and balance of development; the mother in her turn knows instinctively if 'something is wrong inside.' Sometimes such stresses will bring forward the date of birth, and the hapless premature infant then has to struggle with the strange and unnatural demands of the open air. It is as though the baby senses that, even if it is dangerous, the outside world is less hostile than the inimical world inside.

When she is happy and at rest, however, the mother feels her baby's joyous response. Because none of us can consciously remember what it was like to be a baby, the world of the womb is believed to be an ideal one of comfort; the preborn baby lies rocked in fluid, is protected and fed by his mother, feels her presence around him, hears her heartbeat and recognises her voice. If contained safe and warm, he can remain in what Erich Neumann describes as *'the unitary reality of paradise'*, [8] until such time as he is ready to face the stresses of the world, and experiences pain and hunger for the first time.

Some of the great world religions have found ways to describe this paradisiacal state: *'You it was who fashioned my inward parts; you knitted me together in my mother's womb,'* [9] says the Psalmist in the Old Testament, marvelling at God's handiwork. *'I praise you, for you fill me with awe; wonderful you are, and wonderful your works.'* According to the prophet Muhammad: *'Each of you will have had his created existence brought together in his mother's womb, as a drop for forty days, then a leech like clot for the same period, then a piece of flesh for the same period, after which God sends the angel to blow the spirit into him.'* [10] And Sikhs imagine the unborn baby to be spending his time in the womb loving, praising and singing to God, since, being a passive recipient of nutrition and comfort, he is as yet incapable of human love. Whatever the belief, the womb is meant to be the perfect home for the unborn child.

The baby who is born before time, on the other hand, enters a world that is totally inappropriate for his capabilities. It is then the task of all of us – parents, doctors, midwives and nurses working in hospital to create a world that will, at least, present some comforting experiences to mitigate the distress and the pain. Many human preterm babies put up a valiant fight to live against great odds; this fight should be supported and encouraged in every way possible. Some time ago a television programme filmed in a neonatal intensive care unit showed a tiny hand raised amongst the tubes and the wires. It was the hand of a very premature baby in an incubator (himself small enough to fit in the palm of a hand) lifted up as though to say: 'Here I am – please, help me to live!' 'What can you do with such an appeal' said the doctor 'but try your best?'

If the fight is too long and the demands are too strong, however, the fragile baby will give up the struggle and die; nothing we can do will prevent that happening. What we can do, parents and professionals alike, is to mourn for this baby, respect the value of his short life, and allow him to take his place in our memories, our duties, and our families.

References:

1. Bryant, J. *"Anybody seen my baby?"* More issues at the start of life. Lee Abbey, January 2008.

2. Eaton, Gai (1994) *Islam and the Destiny of Man.* The Islamic Text Society, Cambridge.

3. Bagness, C. (1998) *Genetics, the Foetus and our Future.* Hochland & Hochland Ltd., Hale, Cheshire.

4. Harris, J. (1992) *The Value of Life.* Routledge and Kegan Paul plc., London

5. Taylor, J.V. (2004) *The Go Between God.* SCM Press, London

6. Verny, T. with Kelly, J. (1993) *The Secret Life of the Unborn Child.* Summit Books, 1981; reprinted Warner Books, 1993.

7. Chamberlain, D.B. (1994) *The Sentient Prenate: What Every Parent Should Know.* In: The International Journal of Pre- and Perinatal Psychology and Medicine.

8. Neumann, E. (1976) *The Child.* Harper Colophon Books, Harper & Row, New York.

9. Psalm 139. *The Revised English Bible*, Oxford University Press.

10. Hadith: the sayings of the Prophet Muhammad. (1999) *The Abortion Dilemma 2: The mother or the foetus?* IQRA Trust. Science Work Card Series 10.

CHAPTER TWO
THE MOURNING PROCESS

'Death borders upon our birth,
and our cradle stands in the grave.'

Joseph Hall

'Do not go gentle into this good night' says Dylan Thomas, *'Rage, rage against the dying of the light.'* He seems to suggest that those who confront death should fight against it, when they think of lost opportunities and what might have been. It seems weak to just give in, when valuable months can be bought by the struggle to survive. But when death is foreknown and becomes inevitable, the dying sometimes find that feelings of rage can be outgrown and set aside.

Philip Yancey in his book 'Finding God in Unexpected Places' describes a support group for people with life-threatening illnesses. *'For each member of the group, all of life had boiled down to two issues: surviving and, failing that, preparing for death … The members of Make Today Count confronted death because they had no choice. I had expected a mood of great sombreness, but found just the opposite. Tears flowed freely, of course, but these people spoke easily and comfortably about disease and death. Clearly, the group was the one place they could talk openly about such matters.'* [1]

The date of death for the members of the support group was not unknown – it was now. But for those of us for whom there is only uncertainty – today, tomorrow, never – 'death' is not something to welcome with a sigh and a smile. **'Death'** is a heavy word; it has no ring to it, the sound is dead in itself. Many other expressions have been used in order to avoid the word 'death'; 'passed on', 'departed', 'gone to the fuller life', 'gone home' to name but a few. These expressions may be reassuring, especially for friends and relations trying to offer comfort – it is a fact that people surrounding the bereaved will avoid using the word 'death' if they can – but to the bereaved person, 'death' is the only word that has a ring of truth.

Death is a rite of passage. Mourning is the process of passing through this passage from disbelief to acceptance, and since nobody lives forever we must all follow this process at some time or another. The journey is described in a variety of ways, but it is generally accepted that, while mourners may make the journey in their own time and have their own way of passing the milestones, failure to do so may lead to a state of 'pathogenic' grief, an inability to take up life and move on.

Acute grief has been described as *'a sensation of bodily stress coming in waves.'* The mourner does not feel well. There is sleeplessness and loss of appetite; it seems hard to breath because of a choking feeling, a lump in the throat, a need to sigh; there is exhaustion, and a lack of the will to take any positive action; there is loneliness and a feeling of alienation, a sense of unreality and emotional distance from even the closest loved ones. All these intense emotions have to be lived through before mourning can be resolved and life taken up again.

Mourning is an individual process, and nobody should be forced into a ritual before they are ready. However, practical guidelines for helping the bereaved can be based on three premises:

1. The bereaved person is helped to accept the death of a loved one by perceiving its concrete reality.

2. Having acknowledged the external reality of the loss, the bereaved person needs to adapt to it internally through the process of mourning.

3. If the bereaved person fails to accomplish the mourning task, he or she will be unable to resume healthy progressive functioning. [2]

On the way to acceptance of death, the bereaved person must pass through the stages of **disbelief**, **anger**, **guilt**, **inertia**, **grief**, until finally **acceptance** of the reality of death is reached. The initial disbelief may present itself as a period of absolute **denial**, when the bereaved person may retreat behind a shell of non-communication with the outside world as a form of protection against an intolerable truth. At this stage, offers of counselling are often refused and even seen as a form of intrusion on death's privacy.

It may be that this denial does in fact protect the mourner from feelings so strong they appear like a form of madness; sleeplessness, anxiety, fear, anger and a pre-occupation with self may combine to give a sensation of 'going mad', but they are natural feelings and provided they are not stifled and 'pushed down' they will subside over time. The time taken may be vastly different between different people, so offers of comfort and counselling should always be made, even if the mourner may not wish to take up the offer straight away. The newly bereaved feel isolated, as though they and their grief are alone in the world; if at first they seem withdrawn, shunning everyone around them, there will come a time when they will feel the need to come out from behind their protective shell and take up the world and its problems again – and at this moment they will need the support of others.

This mourning process is appropriate for sorrow at the passing of older persons, but it is complicated by the special circumstances surrounding the death of a preborn or newborn baby; namely, that the parents are mourning someone they have not been given the time to recognise, and who has never had the chance to lead a conscious life. Grief is compounded by a sense of futility; it is against the natural order of things that life should end before it has even begun. The baby is a symbol of creativity, the child a symbol of potential growth, so parents not only lose the present, but the future as well.

Peggy Orenstein described her confusion at this dilemma following a miscarriage: *'Social personhood may be distinct from biological and legal personhood, yet the zing of connection between me and my embryo felt startlingly real, and at direct odds with everything I believe about when life begins. Nor have those beliefs – a complicated calculus of science, politics and ethics – changed. I tell myself this wasn't a person. It wasn't a child. At the same time, I can't deny that it was* something. *How can I mourn what I don't believe existed.'*[3]

Mourning the death of a baby

The problem facing parents of a baby who dies before or just after birth is they are in fact mourning for someone who has never lived, who has neither past nor future. Such a death is an affront to the rituals of death. How can family members, friends and neighbours comfort the parents for the loss of someone they have never known? What words can they find for such an occasion? Only too often the chosen words are the wrong ones.

> There is a story of a man who failed to find the right words, when, after many years, he encountered an old friend in the street: 'How is your wife?' he asked. 'She is in Heaven,' his friend replied. 'Oh, I am sorry!' stammered the man. Then feeling this was perhaps not the right thing to say he struggled on, 'I mean, I'm so glad!' Realising this was even worse he tried again, 'Well, what I really mean is – I'm surprised!' This story illustrates the difficulties of finding words of commiseration that are acceptable, and do not appear too banal.

In the book 'Continuing Bonds', Dennis Klass tells the story of a mother who found a complete change of perception from her community when her newborn baby died shortly after birth:

'When she was expecting, everyone told her that this was the most blessed of life's events and that her baby was a new person, a unique individual, different from anyone else. She was told this new person would change her life forever.

'And yet when this most blessed and unique person dies, everybody acts like it's nothing: "Oh well, better luck next time"; "its better he died before you got to know him"; "You'll have more babies" ... So parents who lose a baby will generally try to hide their feelings of grief from others for fear of ridicule, disapproval, or stern lectures about how lucky they are – to have other children or the ability to have new (and obviously improved) babies. [4]

In an attempt to be kind following the death of a baby, people mistakenly try to follow a well-practised formula in attempts to belittle the loss. Someone may try to console the mother by a sort of 'magical repair', saying that she 'can soon have another', or that the death was 'all for the best'. But this is not what the mother wants to hear. At this moment she is aching for the loss of this baby and does not want to think of replacing her with another; nor does she think her loss was 'all for the best'. She mourns the life that never was, the future that does not exist, and she wonders at the wasted hopes. What was the purpose of the months of waiting and preparing for her coming child; and where is that child now, who never felt her, looked at her, smelled her, sucked at her breast?

Disbelief/denial: The mother says: 'This can't have happened to me.' Where is this baby? She has great difficulty in seeing the lost baby as a person who has existed. The long, often uncomfortable months of pregnancy have ended in nothing; she may feel abandoned, disorientated. Her breasts are uncomfortable with useless milk, her arms ache to embrace, but there is nothing to hold. She may try to pretend to herself that the pregnancy never happened, and this may result in feelings of unaccountable loss years later. The mother needs help to accept the reality of the dead child.

Anger: Anger is a powerful and invigorating emotion, and may help to lift the bereaved person from disbelief and denial. But anger is also a destructive emotion, particularly if it is directed at an imaginary source. The parents are angry at the circumstances that have brought about the death of their baby, and will search for someone or something to blame: 'Why has this happened to me? Whose fault is it?' This anger may lead to wild accusations and insults that are hard for others to bear. Parents may rail against the apparent unconcern of partners, relations, friends, and of course, the supreme indifference of God. How could an all-loving God allow such things to happen?

Rage is an expense of energy, but if it is allowed to take its furious course it will finally burn out; and then perhaps that energy can be harnessed to something more constructive. Partners, relations and friends need at first to be receptive and attentive; argument and reasoning will not help distraught parents.

Doctors and nurses also need great patience with parents who, in their anger, often say hurtful things that are hard to forget. Anger and insult have to be tolerated and forgiven; an angry response may give temporary relief to hurt feelings, but will be self-defeating in the long term. If the anger is justified, it will not help if the hospital team try to conceal blame or brush it away; there will be the need for a sympathetic ear to begin with, and later for honest discussion between all concerned – and, most important of all, a telling of truth.

Nobody wants to compound the grief of parents by leaving them with memories of anger and aggression. Parents can express an enduring anger, never resolved, dating from as much as twenty years from the loss of their baby. **Both** parents need to express their anger before they can experience the pain of grief.

Guilt: 'It must be my fault. What did I do wrong?' Sadly, parents who lose babies always seem to feel that somehow they must be to blame, whether it is by some incident during pregnancy or by some personal neglect. Frequently there is a sense of failure, as though they are ashamed at not achieving a healthy, living child. Usually there is no justification, but sometimes, of course, the reason for the guilt is very real, as in those mothers who smoke heavily or are drug addicts, or have neglected their own health. In these cases, once the problem is identified, something can be done to resolve it.

Inertia: 'I'm too tired to think – in any case, there's nothing I can do.' The lassitude that overcomes the bereft parents is perhaps the most dangerous part of the mourning process because it saps the strength; and not only the parents but also everyone around them may suffer. Parents feel numb, helpless and inadequate; there is lethargy, a reluctance to take action of any sort. This time is most dangerous for the whole family, as either parent may feel resentful at the listless behaviour of the other (fathers are not exempt from a feeling of helplessness following the death of a baby); and siblings may feel unloved by parents who don't respond to them, and believe themselves to be somehow 'in the way'.

Parents who have reached the stage of inertia need to be helped to move on to full-bodied, painful grief, and for this the baby must have an existence; she must become 'real' to them.

There are many ways to help parents come to understand that they have lost a person who has lived, even if for a short time, and who can be mourned; details of these ways are discussed in the last chapter of this book, 'Moving On.'

Grief, leading to acceptance: 'I will never forget this baby; she will always be part of me, but I am ready to take up my life without her.' The death of a newborn baby is not 'natural' – babies are not supposed to die – but there is nothing unnatural about grief. All of us have lost people we love at some time or another.

Mutual grief can draw couples together, particularly at first, but later on problems can arise if they are not completely open with one another. The mourning process varies in length between different people; one partner will usually become reconciled before the other, and this causes tensions unless it is understood. Within couples there can be misunderstandings as one recovers from the loss and takes up his or her life, while the other remains deep in mourning. Both parents need great patience with each other.

It is important that neither parent should feel constrained to conceal their emotions, but people do not all grieve in the same way. Some may sense that they are expected to demonstrate emotions they do not at the moment feel, or are too shocked and numb to express, and this will increase their frustration, anger and bitterness. Other parents may believe it is wrong to inflict their grief on the people around them, particularly other children, but this is a mistake, as we shall see later. These people will attempt to conceal their grief at considerable cost to themselves, and by so doing put a strain on their relationship with their partner. Great patience is needed by everyone concerned, but once the stages of the mourning process are safely passed, both mother and father can come to the realisation that the lost baby was a real person, who need not be forgotten, but who can be mourned as a permanent part of the family.

References:

1.   Yancey, P. (1995) *Finding God in Unexpected Places*. Hodder & Stoughton, London.

2.   Furman, E. (1976) Comment in: *Maternal-Infant Bonding* (eds. M.M.Klaus & J.H.Kennell). C.V.Mosby, St. Louis.

3.   Orenstein, P. (2002) *Mourning my Miscarriage*. The New York Times Magazine, April 21.

4.   Klass, D. (1996) The Deceased Child in the Psychic and Social Worlds of Bereaved Parents During the Resolution of Grief. In: *Continuing Bonds* (Eds. Klass D.; Silverman P.R.; & Nickman, S.L.), Taylor & Francis, London.

PART II

DEATH BEFORE LIFE

The Quilt

'I don't know what to do with the half-finished Noah's ark quilt.
I can't finish it, but I can't throw it away either. It was for my
baby. I can't bear that she will never sleep under it. Maybe
someday I'll know how to deal with it, but for now I don't know
what to do.'

:

CHAPTER THREE
DEATH BEFORE BIRTH

'Already the baby was a reality to me; not just a mass of cells, or even a foetus: it was our child. Already I had dreams for the future...'

Karen Holford: 'The Loneliest Grief'

Most women long for their unborn babies, and already love them even if they are still unseen. They delight in the first signs of energy and movement felt within; they encourage partners and other children to 'listen in'. In the clinic, listening to heartbeats, they watch with anticipation signs of life on the scan. It is easy to believe in the marvel of developing intelligence when thumbs find their way to mouths, and limbs adjust themselves to the shape of the womb. Even with the frequent discomforts of pregnancy, women look forward to becoming mothers, as they sense the growth and advance within them. The developing baby is a creation of their own, nourished and protected by their bodies; still a part of them. For this reason, many women view miscarriage as a mutilation, as if part of their own body is stripped away. What was it all for?

Anger and **guilt** are the predominant feelings of mothers who lose babies before birth, even if the pregnancy is not far advanced; both these feelings may well be directed at a very real cause.

Anger

There is a tendency to belittle the anguish caused by a miscarriage. Predominantly, the anger of mothers who miscarry is due to the unfeeling behaviour or seeming indifference of the people around them, whether from their own partner, family and friends, or from professional people concerned in their care. People are embarrassed by miscarriage; they don't know how to respond, so they either say nothing or essay a false cheerfulness. It is not helpful to suggest to a mother who is mourning the death of her unborn child: 'It is probably all for the best.' How can losing a baby be for the best? Even if there was a weakness in the fetus, immediately after the loss is not the time to suggest that all was for the best. The mother is not likely to agree with that; the lost baby is the baby she wants.

Those trying to give comfort to the parents of lost babies must be very careful not to say anything that might endanger their religious faith. Karen Holford is a Christian. She found the one Job's comforter remark most difficult to deal with was: *'God obviously never meant that child to be.'* If God had never intended her to have her baby, Karen felt, why did He let her become pregnant in the first place? The remark was one of the commonest that came her way, and by putting God in such a negative light made it even more difficult for her to come to terms with her loss. She took comfort from God's promise for the future in Isaiah chapter 65: *'See, I am creating new heavens and a new earth! … No child there will ever again die in infancy'*, even if for her that future had not arrived.[1]

A mother who has just lost a baby through miscarriage is not looking for advice; and one piece of advice she does not need is that she should straight away attempt another pregnancy. This may be a temptation, but to become pregnant in order to recapture the lost child is not the route to happy motherhood. The new 'replacement' child may well be resented because it is not identical to the first, and any consequent failure in attachment may leave lasting scars (see Chapter Four).

In fact, there is no need to depend on philosophy, psychology, uplifting morality or wise old saws when accompanying someone in their grief. Very often the simplest ways are best. Christine O'Keeffe Lafser describes how she was helped by sisterly love: *'My sister looks at me with kindness and listens. She holds me, and we cry together. With her I can let go and sob. Then, when our tears are spent, she says something that makes us both laugh. I find comfort in her arms, if only for a little while.'* [2]

Many women who have experienced failed pregnancies that have ended in miscarriage can remember anger and resentment years later. This has usually been due to people connected with them at the time, including hospital staff, ignoring the event as if it was a trivial incident – in fact, as if nothing had happened. It may be difficult to understand how a woman in the early stages of pregnancy can grieve for a child she has never seen or heard, and who may not even be properly formed, but lack of understanding will leave the woman with a bottled up resentment that may surface after decades.

> Martin came to repair a television set. While working, he confessed how, for many years of marriage, he misunderstood how much his wife had suffered following a miscarriage; how he had no patience with her – thought she should 'pull herself together'. Many years later, during a trivial argument, all this came out in a spate of rage; wiser then, he was able to put things right.

Looking back to the importance of words, it infuriates mothers to hear their lost children referred to as 'fetuses'; to most mothers who miscarry their babies are not fetuses, no matter how immature. I remember one occasion, at a bereavement conference in Bristol to which parents had been invited, a funeral director spoke of the respect his company had for the bereaved. He was obviously sensitive and caring, but all the time he referred to babies lost before they were born as 'fetuses'; he was totally astonished by the wave of hostility that swept the audience. Technically, as we have seen, the preborn baby **is** a fetus, but to parents he is a baby in the making; why not acknowledge him as such?

Gender also is a factor; babies are not 'neuter'; sexual identity appears early in pregnancy, and it is easier to mourn for a boy or a girl than it is for an 'it'.

Many mothers resent the fact that they have not been allowed to see their baby; they are left wondering what sort of monstrosity has been hidden from them. Parents should ask to see the baby if they so wish, even if there is a malformation; very often the imagination will paint a picture far blacker than the reality. Even preborn babies have an identity, and it will help parents if they can have this identity confirmed; to deny them the right to see and touch their own child is, in a way, to deprive them of their own identity as parents. On the other hand, they should never be forced to look at their baby if they cannot bear the thought of it.

Sometimes, if there has been mismanagement, parents have good reason to be angry. In this case a 'conspiracy of silence' will be futile; parents who want to know the truth will insist until they find out, and the effort and energy they have to expend in order to do so will leave them with lasting resentment. The parents will need to discuss their complaint with a senior member of the neonatal team, someone they already know and trust. At such a time, anger and insult must be tolerated. It may help if the parents are encouraged to talk about their anger and give it a name – frustration, disappointment, or a feeling of helplessness, perhaps. Angry parents in their first grief should be listened to with compassion and without argument.

Guilt

Mothers who miscarry are likely to feel guilt, very often for no good reason. The mother feels guilty because she has failed to 'house' the baby until he is ready to be born. This may be due to reasons beyond her control, such as infection, malfunction of the uterus, or abnormality in the fetus. The loss is perceived as an injury, a blow to the woman's self-esteem and sense of power. In some cases the mother may in fact be resenting an unwanted pregnancy, or she may become weary of the burden of pregnancy itself.

Guilt may be justified, if the mother continues to smoke and drink, and has neglected to care for herself during the pregnancy. If there are social problems, now is the time to sort them out.

Guilt, as well as anger, can be carried through the years, never to be forgotten. This is hard to cope with – what cure is there for guilt? If the reasons for the miscarriage are clear, learning all there is to know about the circumstances of the death may mitigate guilt. Full knowledge in this respect may also help the parents to avoid a repetition.

It may help to know that many share 'guilt', and to talk to other women who have been through the same or similar experiences can be healing. There are organisations that provide women with the opportunity to share their difficulties and experiences with others; a list of these will be found at the end of the book.

Miscarriage

Miscarriages are unforeseen and, besides the shock and grief felt by the parents, they are a source of immense disappointment and frustration. The bereaved sometimes find it helpful to put their feelings on paper by keeping a diary or by writing letters to the deceased. Following miscarriage, Karen Holford wrote a letter to her baby: *'I felt totally rejected by you. I felt I had given so much of myself and my heart to you and you were just throwing it all back in my face, and walking out… I was angry, hurt and violated… We could never cuddle you and say goodbye properly. Instead there was emptiness, tears and fears.'* [1]

Abortion

This is not the place for a discussion on ethics, but it is not possible to discuss death before birth without mentioning abortion. Abortion may appear at first to relieve the pressures of an unwanted pregnancy, but in the long term it is frequently seen to be the cause of stress and anxiety, a traumatic experience whose destructive elements remain within a person for months, frequently for years. It would seem that to procure an abortion might only replace one pain with another. Gloria Swanson, glamorous actress of the '30s and '40s, wrote about an abortion she had procured at the height of her career: *The greatest regret of my life has always been that I didn't have my baby... Nothing in the whole world is worth a baby. I realized it as soon as it was too late and I never stopped blaming myself* [3]   The actress Patricia Neal in her autobiography 'As I Am' also wrote about an abortion she had had many years before: *For over 30 years, alone in the night, I cried... If I had only one thing to do over in my life, I would have that baby.* [4]

Both parents can suffer guilt over an abortion procured because of an unwanted pregnancy, and this guilt may remain to damage their lives over decades. Unfortunately, many parents of aborted children think they have no right to be sad. In modern society, women are not encouraged to reflect on the abortion and its physical and psychological effect on them. They are supposed to forget about it as soon as they close the clinic door behind them, and get on with their lives as if nothing has happened.

But something has happened. The aborted fetus may indeed be 'just a cluster of cells', but to the mother it is an unwanted baby; it was the coming baby she feared. Whatever the rights and wrongs, she feels deep within herself that she has taken a life, and that life part of her own body. It is understandable that women should suffer feelings of sorrow, self-loathing and guilt following such an act, and it is not helpful to pretend, as some do, that those suffering post-abortion depression must have been mentally unstable beforehand.

If the child is unwanted, for whatever reason, young women are frequently put under enormous pressure to undergo an abortion by parents, partners, friends, colleagues, and health care professionals. But there is little support for any subsequent feelings of guilt, which sometimes doubles the guilt felt. Many women conceal their feelings for years, and when eventually they speak they tell, with tears, of the isolation they felt, alone with their guilt and their sense of loss.

> Dominique became pregnant while waiting for her divorce to come through, so she procured an abortion. Some years later she became pregnant by her second husband and delivered a little girl. To her horror, this baby was diagnosed as having a heart abnormality incompatible with life. Dominique sat watching her baby die; she told us later she was convinced this was God's punishment for her previous abortion, and no amount of explaining and consoling would shake her in this belief. The baby died, and Dominique remained convinced she had been responsible for the deaths of two children.

On the other hand, there are always two people to be considered in a pregnancy; an unwanted pregnancy brought to term can also cause endless pain and bitterness for both mother and child. Here again, parents and professionals sometimes put great pressure on an already troubled girl to have the baby she fears. Should the hapless teenager live her whole life with the living reminder of her mistake, (*although a great many do, ultimately without regret) or the victim of rape or incest be faced with a lifetime's reminder of her pain? And how does the unwanted child grow, knowing he is not only not loved, but resented?

> Sean never knew who his father was, although his education was paid for by him. But from the time Sean

could first understand speech, his mother hammered into him that he had 'ruined her life.' This he heard repeatedly down the years (I heard her myself). By the time he was forty-five years old, he saw himself as a complete failure. He took no care of himself, suffered from tuberculosis, was an addicted gambler and alcoholic, but in spite of the fact that his mother, every time she saw him, could still never resist reminding him how he had ruined her life, he never neglected or abandoned her. Basically he was a sweet man, worthy of love, but he spent his life craving for the love he never received. Sean's mother was Irish, a devout Roman Catholic; did she ever regret abortion had never been a possibility for her?

In the United States, Project Rachel is a support organisation run by the Roman Catholic Church for the parents of aborted babies, where they can pour out their feelings to a listening and compassionate ear. There is great need for such support groups, and for recognition that many such parents are in fact left in deep distress, and should be allowed to grieve without feeling they have no right to do so.

Referring to the anthropologist Linda Layne, Peggy Orenstein says: '*new technologies and better medical care encourage us to confer "social personhood" on the fetus with greater intensity and at an ever-earlier stage... women confide in family and friends and begin to sort through names. In an era of vastly reduced infant mortality, they assume all will go well. "When it doesn't" Peggy Orenstein quotes Linda Layne, "the very people participating with us in the construction of this new social person... suddenly revoke that personhood like nothing ever happened."'* [5] This is not helpful to bereaved parents; when rejoicing over a pregnancy turns to grief over a lost child, it is hurtful if family and friends behave as though nothing has happened.

An embryo/fetus is not just 'a bunch of cells'; he is also a person in the making, developing very fast and with great energy, learning and growing inside the womb until he is old enough to breath in the world outside. Parents suffering the loss of a preborn baby should not be made to feel that the miscarried or aborted pregnancy is just a trivial incident to be swept under the carpet. This preborn baby deserves respect; he may have died, but he has also lived, and may be mourned and resigned to memories, as with other departed loved ones.

---

*Some years ago there was a programme on BBC Radio Four concerning teenagers and their problems. Some young girls were speaking about a local society they belonged to which gives support to teenage parents, boys and girls. Without exception, the girls told of their pleasure in their babies, how they managed to combine continuing their education and being good mothers – **with the support they needed from the society**.

The girls also without exception explained how they had been offered abortion by the professionals to whom they had gone for diagnosis and advice. Without exception they were quite adamant that their pregnancy signified 'a baby' to them, and that a baby was what they were going to have. Even given that such programmes tend to be biased one way or another, and many girls may feel quite differently, this was encouraging to hear.

References:

1. Holford, K. (1994) *The Loneliest Grief.* Autumn House Publications, Grantham

2. O'Keeffe Lafser, C. (1998) *An Empty Cradle, A Full Heart.* Loyola Press, Chicago.

3. Swanson, G. (1980) *Swanson on Swanson.* Random House, New York.

4. Neal, P. (1988) *As I Am.* Simon and Schuster, New York.

5. Orenstein, P. (2002) *Mourning my Miscarriage.* The New York Times Magazine, April 21.

CHAPTER FOUR
DEATH AT BIRTH

'How anxious I was for the pregnancy to be over. How impatient I was for each day to pass. Little did I know that those were the only days I would have with you. Why did I wish them away instead of savoring each moment we had together?'

Christine O'Keeffe Lafser: An Empty Cradle, A Full Heart.

Shock, **disbelief**, and **anger** are the feelings that predominate when a baby is born already dead, or only to die. Pregnancy is a time when dreams are realistic; dreams such as these are most frequently fulfilled. It will take a long time for the parents to accept that the pregnancy has ended in death. Unfortunately, and only too often, the loss of a baby is not seen as a serious bereavement; as in the case of miscarriage, family, friends and neighbours sometimes pretend that nothing has happened. No one wishes to mention the dead baby, either for fear of stirring up sad memories, or from embarrassment. 'The worst of it was,' said one mother whose baby died at birth 'I saw my friends cross over the street in order not to speak to me.' This panic behaviour is understandable, but it is very hurtful to parents, and is not easily forgotten.

Shock

The brutal suddenness of death is a terrible shock to parents who have endured the discomfort of a nine-month pregnancy in the happy expectation of taking home with them a beautiful, healthy child. How is it possible that, between one moment and the next as it seems, the pain that is intended to lead to relief, joy, exultation, turns to confusion, quickly followed by emptiness? The bewildered woman who was expecting to be able to call herself a mother looks down to see hurried movements, a bundling away of products, eyes that will not meet her own. Her partner, if he is present, will have been a witness to haste, anxiety, and a desperate urgency. He will find that he is forgotten; sometimes an attempt will be made to hurry him away. There is rarely time for explanation at such moments, so the couple will not have any idea what is going on.

A crucial time is the immediate period following the birth. Professionals in the hurry and bustle to clean away the tragedy of the dead child may forget that the child's mother and father are present, desperately trying to understand what is happening.

> Clarice remembers how twenty-five years ago she gave birth to twins, born at term but both born dead. She remembers looking up to see the midwife hurry away, clutching something wrapped in a towel – not a limb showed. Not much was said, no explanation of the deaths followed. She was wheeled on a stretcher to the post-natal ward, where she remained, childless, surrounded by happy mothers talking and laughing, breast-feeding, changing and caring for their living babies. Clarice still feels a choking sensation when she remembers that time. She has not forgotten.

The abrupt change of circumstances is monumental for the would-be parents; they are suddenly left with nothing. They will return home to face preparations that are now useless; probably even inconvenient, now there is no one to sleep in the cot, look at the mobiles, make up stories about the wallpaper, and play with the toys. Many parents who have experienced the death of an infant at birth refuse to prepare their home at the next pregnancy, preferring to offer a last minute rush as a hostage to fortune.

Disbelief

The father, if he has witnessed the birth, will have been aware of the events leading to the death even if he has not understood them. The mother herself, who has put all her concentration and energy into the labour, will find it hard to believe what has happened to her.

There was a time when death was the common outcome of a pregnancy. Women were prepared to lose a child, and frequent pregnancies could equally frequently be expected to end in relatively small families. Some women lost every baby they conceived, and still went on trying for a living child. Queen Anne, for example, lost eight babies; only one survived, and he was hydrocephalic and died young.

These days, however, pregnancies are usually expected to be accomplished successfully and in triumph. Death that is unexpected is usually more traumatic than one that has been half anticipated, and can be perceived as an overwhelming loss. The resolution of such grief may well take much longer; a 'shadow grief' may persist as a lingering but transient sadness years after the loss occurred.

The expected baby may have been a 'dream baby', but the pregnancy was after all a real one; the baby born was flesh and blood. It is a fatal mistake to hurry away the dead baby at this time, particularly if the mother is not allowed to see her later on. How can she resolve her confusion between the perfect baby who existed only in her imagination and the baby that existed within her body, even if she was not born alive? In the case of death at birth, it is important that the parents should be able to hold, bathe, and dress the baby if they so wish. At least this is some service they can perform, some care they can give, which might mitigate the sense of failure.

It is important at this stage to emphasise that it is **never safe to make assumptions!** There are parents who may not feel able to hold their dead baby, or even to see her; it may exacerbate the pain if they feel under pressure to do so. The parents should be gently encouraged to say exactly what they wish to be done. Even if they are too hurt and upset to see and hold the baby at the time, photographs can be taken and kept for the parents if they should need them later.

Anger

'I went into the delivery room looking forward to holding my baby,' says the mother. 'Now I have nothing to hold; did you kill my baby?' How else but with anger can one cope with such an ordeal? After the shock and disbelief are passed, anger is predominant. No baby dies during the birth process without reason. A couple, who enter the maternity hospital convinced that the happy day has arrived which they will be celebrating for years to come as their child's birthday, are not going to accept a dead baby without question. What happened? After all, someone must be to blame, and it is unlikely to be the woman herself, who has trusted her body to professional obstetricians and midwives.

Many things can go wrong; the baby may have turned into an awkward position within the womb, or may be exhausted from a prolonged labour, but skilled medical staff can resolve even unpreventable problems, such as a cord around the neck. Professionals in the maternity services, using highly technical modern equipment, are expert in recognising danger signals before they threaten the safety of mother and child. Even if there are always circumstances that no one could have foreseen, in a hospital setting there is a choice of ways in which emergencies can be met.

At first, the parents are not likely to enquire too closely into the details of the failed birth, but later on there is a place for a full and open discussion. Whatever the circumstances and whoever has made a mistake, 'cover-up' will not do. If there have been errors, these should be admitted. When such cases have come to court and compensation has to be paid, most couples find some relief in feeling that justice has been done. The money is not important; what is important is that a case can be closed.

Mistakes are made, with dreadful consequences. Those responsible who are honestly sorry can be forgiven, and I believe parents often do not realise what heartache medical failure can bring the professional. Failure to assist at a successful birth is not always due to incompetence or carelessness. The truth is that human error on the part of doctors and nurses can lead to loss of life, a fact they have always at the back of their minds as they work, and which does not make their lives any easier.

Angry parents need to be led through their anger. This can be done by:

- *listening* to the parents without interrupting

- *looking* at the parents while they are speaking

- *not attempting to justify* at this stage any action taken, even if the anger is a blind hitting out at the nearest person; justification is not appropriate at this time – it will simply exacerbate the anger

- *sympathising* with the feeling of anger, without apportioning blame

- *never answering anger with anger*. It is important to remain warm and friendly; the anger is rarely personal. Later on the person may be sorry, and it will have been important to maintain a good relationship

- *being patient.* Anger usually does not last, and may be regretted later

- *keep the parents informed* – there is nothing worse than the feeling that people are keeping information from you

- *attempting to moderate conflict* between the partners, if necessary. The anger sometimes erupts between the two who are the most hurt, and can lead to breakdown in relationships

- *taking action* to put right misconceptions; investigating alleged errors in practice.[1]

These are the words of a bereaved mother, trapped in a hospital room following the death of her baby:

> 'It would have helped me, just at that particular time, if I could have done something violent to express how violent I felt. I was cooped up in my hospital room, feeling physically very weak, consumed with anger and hate. I hated my baby because it had failed me. I hated my breasts for producing milk when there was no baby to feed. I hated the doctor who had failed to revive my baby after she was born. I hated all those women who had live, healthy babies to feed and care for. I hated the sad faces of people who came to see me. Most of all, I hated God for letting this awful, unimaginable thing happen…'[1]

Following the shock and disbelief, feelings that paralyse the bereaved person, anger is at least an active emotion. Perhaps it is healthy that it comes at this time, stirring up the will to move, to 'do something', even if the something is violent. With patience and understanding, anger can be dissipated and the strong feelings can be used to better purpose. But patience, understanding and honesty in dealings with the parents are needed; if buried, anger can remain unresolved and resurface years later to no good purpose. Better that anger is allowed to express itself and run its course, than be suppressed and boiling away within forever.

'Replacement'

Parents of babies who die before, during or after birth frequently hear these words of consolation: 'After all, dear, you can always have another.' Many parents resent this remark and feel that nothing can replace the baby they lost, but sometimes the feeling is that a new baby will somehow ease the pain. We now know how unwise it is to rush into another pregnancy before grief for the lost baby has drawn to its conclusion, and the fact of death is acknowledged and accepted. 'Replacement' is an ugly word. How can a child understand its existence as a substitute for someone else? If it is loved, the love is 'lent' by another child. If it is not loved, it is because its individuality means it can never become a replica of the lost child.

The parents of a dead child who try to replace it with another make a grave mistake. They wake up to find their first child is still gone – unmourned, because they have not given themselves time, in their frenzy of grief, to complete their mourning. So the bereavement goes on and on, a bitter wound that anger and guilt will never allow to resolve. And the new child is resented as a changeling, a sign of failed promise.

Martha's mother lost a little girl at two years, and immediately tried for another, whom she hoped would be exactly the same as the first. Another little girl was duly born, but she was small and dark, totally unlike the rosy, blonde baby who had died. Martha's mother was bitterly disappointed, and allowed Martha to know it. The little girl was made aware that her mother's love had been totally given to the first child, and she herself had failed to fill the gap. She was a woman grown, with children of her own, before she was able to come to terms with the feeling of

73

being not herself but a 'replacement'; even then she never felt her mother had quite forgiven her.

Two lives were soured by this rush into pregnancy before the lost child had been laid to rest. A lost child cannot be forgotten – but nor can it ever be replaced; it must be allowed to die. Only then can the confused and lonely 'replacement' child find its place in the hearts of its parents.

References:

1.   Sparshott, M. *The Angry Parent.* (1996) In: *Relating to the Relatives: breaking bad news, communication and support,* by Brewin, T. & Sparshott, M. Radcliffe Medical Press, Oxford.

CHAPTER FIVE
DEATH AFTER BIRTH

'Even if you have logical answers, they don't address the real why. Why me? Why now? Why this innocent babe? ... I think the search for the answer to that why – the search for the very meaning of life – is a lifetime's work.'

Nancy Kohner & Alix Henley: When a Baby Dies.

Death that occurs shortly after birth commits the parents to a time of intense anxiety and stress; they do not know, cannot guess the outcome of their child's illness – or they have been forewarned and have to face the dreary time of waiting for the worst thing to happen. Nerves are stretched at this time; it is like an illness for the parents themselves. They must force themselves to believe they are going to lose their baby and prepare themselves for that loss, but they will experience feelings of **anger**, **guilt**, **inertia** and **grief** even before the baby has died. Once again, as in the other cases of perinatal death, they have to face their feelings of failure at not being able to take home the healthy baby of their dreams.

Anger

The parents feel anger at the ruin of their hopes for the coming child. Instead of a living, growing baby they are faced with someone who is fading, slipping backwards, preparing to leave them. They feel cheated of the lost future. At the end of a long life death may be mourned as the loss of a loved one, but that life has at least been lived. What is the point of a baby who is born only to die? It has no meaning. Death is not acceptable at the beginning of life; it is neither fair nor just.

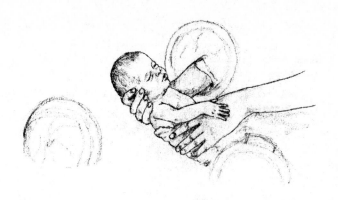

The parents are angry with themselves for their apparent failure as parents. They are angry with the doctors who, surely, could do something to save this life. They are angry with nurses who are touching and caring for a baby that does not belong to them; maybe there is even frustrated rage at treatments performed that must give pain.

Worst of all, the parents cannot help feeling angry with this fragile baby who is yet not a baby; it is as though (like the 'replacement' child) he is a changeling, sent to them out of malice to replace the beautiful dream baby who never came. It is as though they are being required to mourn two babies, the one who never materialised, and the one for whom they can do nothing to hold to life. So anger feeds on anger, and is furnaced by helplessness, frustration and guilt.

Guilt

Parents of babies who die after birth feel guilty because they wonder if they could have done something to prevent the death. Once again, it is the sense of failure that is so painful. Perhaps it is something not right in themselves that has caused the failure to produce a healthy child, and of course this is sometimes the case; it is important for both parents to learn if there is any genetic problem in the family, which has been fatal for the child and might resurface in another pregnancy. As in all cases of early death, existing psychosocial problems need to be sorted out.

Harder to rationalise is the illogical guilt of the mother who feels that it is some action of her own which has caused her to have a sick child. Many young mothers look back over the months of the pregnancy, searching for actions they might have taken which could have led to their baby's weakness. These will not be difficult to find, since any action or non-action can be held to blame. 'Did I not take enough exercise? Should I have stopped walking the dog every day? Was it wrong to make love? Did I eat enough – or too much?' Even more painful are the guilty feelings. 'Was it that day we had the quarrel? Did I moan once too often about being tired? Did I, secretly, somehow wish my baby was not there, and I was young and attractive again?'

Fathers, also, have their share of useless guilt. Perhaps they failed in care of the future mother and baby. Perhaps they felt overburdened by the coming responsibility of a family. Or perhaps they were secretly jealous at having to share the love of their partner. All these feelings of guilt and many more, indeed guilt for almost anything, can bedevil the poor parents trying to cope with grief for their dying child.

Inertia

Parents feel helpless at the sight of their sick child being cared for by others. Every neonatal nurse recognises the sight of the mother sitting by the side of the incubator, peering through the perspex. Sometimes a hand will come out and touch the incubator, as if that was the only contact possible. Such inertia is not helpful, nor is it necessary. In the most severe of illnesses, except when even to touch the baby may be too stressful for him, there are actions the parents should be able to take. Basic nursing procedures, such as nappy changing and tube feeding, can be taught to both parents if they wish to perform them. If parents feel they have something to do, and are actively taking part in their baby's care, this can lift the inertia, and at least give them some memories of having looked after their own child to comfort them later on.

Cherishment

At one time, 'models of nursing' were developed for nurses to use in the clinical field to facilitate holistic care of the patient. In 1990 I developed such a nursing model based on human needs to be used by neonatal nurses caring for sick and preterm babies in hospital.[1,4] This model identified the baby's physical needs and emotional requirements, and included parents in the nursing aim, which was to 'cherish' the baby (Appendix 1). The verb 'cherish' means 'to protect and treat with affection: to nurture, to nurse'. Cherishing their own baby in a neonatal unit can at least reinforce the parental role, if the baby is not too severely ill to support it. Parents sitting by the side of an incubator, watching through the barrier of the transparent cover, become very skilled at reading the good and bad messages sent by the baby. After a time, they also discover the best way to soothe and distract him, to make him comfortable, to ease his pain.

Using categories of environmental disturbance and their treatment, professional and parental caregivers can learn how to balance good and bad experiences: pain with therapy, discomfort with consolation, and disturbance with cherishment[2,4] (Appendix 2). Babies who are not too ill love the sound of the human voice, and will welcome the soft voice of mother and father. Most babies love to hold a finger, and will show this by the way they grip; a star-shaped hand, pushing away rather than clutching, can show this is not welcome.

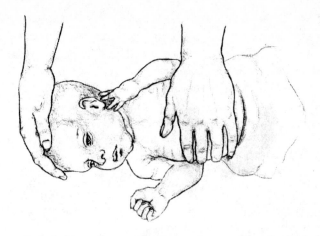

Even babies who are too ill to accept stroking can be held in a way that doesn't require from them any response. This form of touch is **containment**, which calls for the baby to be gently and lightly held, without stroking, with one hand cupping the crown of his head and the other placed over his trunk[3,4] (see illustration). Babies may not be able to speak, but they have their own language; a relaxing of the body and hands and regular breathing will show the touch is accepted. On the other hand, restless movements, uneven breathing or pauses in breathing, together with a change in colour, may show that even this comforting touch is too much.

As soon as the baby is mature enough to be fed orally, even if only by a gastric tube, then the mother's own milk can be used – another important action she can take, especially as no one else can do it! Even before feeding is possible, a breast pad soaked in milk can be placed near the baby's head, which will help to stimulate the sense of smell. And if the baby is well enough, he can be removed from the incubator, even if still dependant on a ventilator for breathing, to be held against the mother's skin; an action that will be good for both. In fact, either parent can do this.

The presence of parents is important to the baby in hospital; they are the ones who will best learn their baby's individual needs. Their concern will lead them to recognise changes in state and behaviour busy nurses and doctors may miss. And it is not only mothers who become skilled at changing and consoling their babies. Fathers may be glad to learn that they are far from being as clumsy as they sometimes fear; on the contrary, most fathers become adept at caring for their babies and are quite capable of sharing in the tasks of parenthood. Parents may believe that, far from being onlookers in the neonatal unit, separated from their own child by the physical barriers of incubators and ventilators and lack of specialist knowledge, their presence is indispensable.

It is hard for parents to endure the time of waiting for their baby to live or die. Babies sometime survive for months of heartbreak, seeming one day to be winning the battle (and they are plucky fighters) and the next to relapse into precarious illness. But at least these parents are, or will have been, parents. At least they have had an actual body, with limbs that move, eyes that see, and a beating heart, to remember and to mourn. It is good for both parents to do as much for their sick baby as possible, even if they accept that the outlook is bleak. Since they are likely to be the ones who spend most of their time by the sides of their babies, they can get to know their likes and dislikes, and can help by recording this for the nurses. There are tables showing the signs of stress and well-being at the back of this book[4] (Appendix 3), together with possible ways to soothe and comfort.

Above all, the parents of a baby who dies after birth are left with memories of that baby, which they will always carry with them and may surface years later. Memories are unavoidable; there will be much pain, but even after such an ordeal, many parents look back with gratitude and warmth – every effort must be made by professional carers to see the memories are not totally negative.

Death with dignity

In the nursing model, last on the list of emotional requirements is the need to 'die with dignity.' When the time comes for the baby to die, both parents will need to be involved. Babies should die in the arms of their parents, whose touch should be the last they feel. Once again it is dangerous to make assumptions, but in more that 20 years of neonatal nursing I have seldom known a couple who did not wish to be with their baby at this time.

Wise doctors and nurses will see that all is arranged; decisions of a withdrawal of treatment should be unanimous, and parents should be given time to understand all that is involved. An agreement as to timing and procedure can usually be reached if parents have the opportunity to assess all the facts and to consult between themselves.

It has been suggested that some parents might wish themselves to discontinue the life-support systems for their own children, but this should be approached with caution – it is difficult enough for the professional carer. Parents could not possibly anticipate the revulsion one feels at doing such a thing, even if one accepts it is entirely necessary. I myself have troubling memories of one such occasion:

> Matthew had lived for three months. Born at 26 weeks gestation, he had taken the usual 'three steps forward to two steps back.' Now it seemed as though he would survive. He was a charming baby, beginning to wake up to the world and look about him with interest. Then he developed necrotising enterocolitis (NEC: a very dangerous condition which destroys the intestine) and did not respond to treatment.
>
> His abdomen became distended, tight as a drum, and it was necessary to insert needles to drain the excess fluid. His breathing failed and he needed to be intubated so that a ventilator could do this work for him. He was in great pain and was given a continuous infusion of morphine, as much

as his weight would allow – but it was not enough. Eventually all of us – doctors, nurses, and parents – saw that he had slipped too far, and all agreed that it was time to let him go; it was, after all, only the breathing ventilator that was keeping him alive.

I was the nurse who removed the tube from his throat, and unlatched the many lines and wires invading his body. He watched me as I removed the tube. This was not the gaze-avoidance of the deeply stressed baby, but a mature gaze. These were the direct and penetrating eyes of knowledge that can be seen on some babies who have endured weeks of invasive procedures in the fight for life. It is hard not to believe he knew what I was doing to him. Then I wrapped him in his own shawl, and took him to be with his parents. He died the same day, a peaceful and dignified death in the arms of his parents – but I see him watching me still. This is not an experience to be wished on any parent.

Death can occur with dignity if the death is foreseen. A private place can be found for the family, and personal desires can be fulfilled. If it is possible, (but only if the parents wish and the baby will not suffer) arrangements can be made to transport the baby to the parents' home, so that he can die in home surroundings. It will in fact be beneficial for everyone if individual requirements can be met to suit the life styles and beliefs of individual parents:

Willow and her partner were a New Age couple whose little daughter Crystal had an illness that was incompatible with life. When the time came for a decision to be made as to whether Crystal should continue breathing with the machine which was keeping her alive, or should be allowed to die peacefully with her parents beside her, Willow and John hesitated. They did not want to make any decision until they had discussed the matter with a mystic, whose gifts, they said, were remarkable. She would know if it was the right thing to do. The consultant responsible for Crystal agreed they should be given the time.

Willow carefully cut a strand of Crystal's hair and the couple took this to the mystic, who kept it beside her overnight. In the morning, she told the parents that it was indeed the right time for Crystal to die; there was no longer any need to prolong her life. This, Willow and John accepted. Crystal was taken from the ventilator and Willow and John kept her with them in their room, alone together. She died peacefully in the early hours of the morning. Willow and John bathed her, dressed her, and prepared her for burial. They then said goodbye to her and went their way.

References

1. Sparshott M. (1990) The Human Touch, *Paediatric Nursing* Vol 2.**5**. 8 -10

2. Sparshott M (1991) Creating a Home for Babies in Hospital, *Paediatric Nursing*, Vol. 3.**8** 20-22

3. Als, H. (1986) A synactive model of neonatal behavioural organization. *Physical and Occupational Therapy in Pediatrics*, **6**, 3 – 53.

4. Sparshott, M. (1997) *Pain, Distress and the Newborn Baby.* Blackwell Science, Oxford.

CHAPTER SIX
THE FAMILY

'And can it be that in a world so full and busy, the loss of one weak creature makes a void in any heart, so wide and deep that nothing but the width and depth of vast eternity can fill it up!'

Charles Dickens: Dombey and Son.

The happiness and stability of communal life depends on the integrity of relationships within a family. Sadly, family unity seems to have lost its importance in these days, when so many problems with young people seem to stem from dysfunctional families. Perhaps it has been a mistake to cry out so loudly for freedom and independence. Freedom is a fine word, but no one can ever be completely free from other people in this world; even anchorites are tied to people by prayer. Nor does independence help when someone is facing grief for the loss of a loved one. Some may seek for solitude in grief, but the knowledge that there are friends and family about them, grieving with them and for them, can be a great support. No one should have to be alone at such a time.

When a baby dies, the needs of other members of the family should not be forgotten in the surge of sympathy felt for the mother of the child. 'The family' can be considered either as the nuclear family of parents and siblings, or the extended family that includes grandparents and other relatives. Nowadays family units tend to be complex; not always do they consist of husband and wife with their children. Frequently the mother's present partner may not be the father of the child, and this can create an imbalance in grieving; stepbrothers and sisters can either be stimulating and enlarging, or can create disunity within the group. The death of a baby can be a uniting factor, as the family is drawn together for mutual support, or it can be divisive, as family members resent the concentration of attention on the one dead child.

One family found it was both strengthened and disturbed by the death of a baby. Becky and Cora are mother and daughter; Cora is the oldest of six siblings, not all from the same father. Some of the stepchildren resented the presence of the new baby, feeling they had enough problems as stepbrothers and sisters without adding yet another child to the family. This left them feeling guilty after the baby's death. All the children grieved, but the stepsiblings had lost their own mother to cancer some years before and believed the whole family to be under a curse.

Becky, in denial, couldn't be bothered with anyone, so she pushed all responsibility onto Cora, who was then seventeen. Cora found some solace in helping her mother and caring for the rest of the family – 'it grew me up' – and this she believes brought mother and daughter closer together. Cora tells how people said to them: 'It gets easier as time goes by'. At the time she thought 'Yeah, right, how can it', because at that moment she thought the whole world had ended and she felt like giving up. As time went by, she found grief easier to bear – but Becky said that for her there

88

was no healing. However, day by day she too became accustomed to the pain.

Becky didn't want counselling as she felt no one could help her who had 'not been through it'; she sought for help from others who had shared the same experience. And she found comfort within her own family. Cora says: 'You never forget and you will always have bad days. But I just give thanks because I will always be glad that my cheeky girl came to stay even if it was just for three months.' [1]

Grief is a great catalyst, and can deepen and strengthen personal relationships to the ultimate good of everyone concerned.

The father

Studies have shown that fathers experience intense feelings of loneliness, isolation, and meaninglessness following the death of their child.[2] 'I soon realised that fathers are not supposed to have emotions', was the complaint of one father, Hay.[3] The stereotyped image of Father as the great breadwinner, the rock and stay, lives on to this day, and blocks many men from relieving their pent-up feelings. There are a number of problems specific to the father:

- Whatever he feels, he is expected to maintain his masculine role

- He is faced with disruption of the home

- He is responsible for maintaining the household routine – care of the other children, grandparents to reassure and satisfy, friends to keep informed, etc.

- He may be shamed at feelings of inadequacy, even fear of death

- He must contend with the practical responsibilities associated with the birth and death of a baby – what procedures must he follow, what papers must he sign?

- He may have financial worries

- He may feel the necessity to conceal his anxieties in the work place; indeed, he may be expected to do so

- Sometimes, he may be jealous of losing the attention of his wife or partner.[4]

For the father as well as the mother, the routines of life are disrupted by the birth and death of a baby; he may have difficulty in understanding the depth of grief and guilt that absorbs his partner, while for him life must go on. It is natural for the distressed woman to turn to her partner at this time, but this throws a strain on him. He needs to express his own feelings of grief, guilt and fear, but he may be prevented from doing so by seeing his role as one who must be stalwart: 'Not once did anyone ask how I was feeling,' said Hay, 'and I would have loved for someone to have said just once "and how are you"?' [3]

Anger at being helpless is the predominant emotion for many bereaved fathers. They feel they should somehow have prevented the tragedy. In her book 'Crucial Decisions at the Beginning of Life', Hazel McHaffie traces the experiences of over 100 families who have lived through the loss of a baby. This is how one father described his frustration at helplessness: 'That's what hurt me more than anything, because you can't **do** anything. If anything's ever happened to me before it's always been something you could do something about. Because I couldn't do anything about it that was worse – it was a strange feeling.' [5]

Many fathers find that continuing or returning to work helps them to keep things in perspective, although they perceive themselves as being less efficient and competent for a time. The father of a preterm baby explained: "My mind wasn't as fit and sharp as it was previously. I think mentally I took a very large knock and it took me a long time to get over that... it was a confidence dent."

Fathers may find some solace in action; for instance, helping to carry the coffin at the funeral may feel like a 'last task' they are performing for their child.

Fathers, as well as mothers, sometimes find help in writing. Janet Goodall, in her chapter 'Grieving Parents, Grieving Children' in 'Representations of Childhood Death', describes how the Dean of St. Paul's, W.R. Inge, a man *'outwardly aloof and apparently unfeeling,'* prefaced his 'Personal Religion and the Life of Devotion' (1924) with a Latin poem commemorating his much-loved little daughter Margaret; *'it is significant that this austere scholar found Latin the only possible medium for his outburst of grief.'* [6] Rabbi Harold Kushner lost his son Aaron two days after his fourteenth birthday, but he and his wife had been aware of his inevitable suffering and early death since he was three years old; Aaron suffered from progeria, 'rapid ageing'. Rabbi Kushner wrote a book about his experience, 'When Bad Things Happen to Good People.' In it he says: *'I knew then that one day I would write this book. I would write it out of my own need to put into words some of the most important things I have come to believe and know. And I would write it to help other people who might one day find themselves in a similar predicament.*[7]

The cruel and protracted death of Aaron contradicted everything Harold Kushner had been taught. *'I could only repeat over and over again in my mind, "this can't be happening. It is not how the world is supposed to work." Tragedies like this were supposed to happen to selfish, dishonest people whom I, as a rabbi, would then try to comfort by assuring them of God's forgiving love. How could it be happening to me, to my son, if what I believed about the world was true?'* He finishes the introduction to his book by firmly stating: *'This is [Aaron's] book, because any attempt to make sense of the world's pain and evil will be judged a success or failure based on whether it offers an acceptable explanation of why he and we had to undergo what we did. And it is his book in another sense as well – because his life made it possible, and because his death made it necessary.'*

A different form of understanding was expressed in the fictional TV series of 'Silent Witness' (strangely – or perhaps not so strangely – profound wisdom can sometimes surface in such stories). This episode told the story of a young girl whose murdered body was found naked in the snow on a mountain top, many years after she had gone missing. The mother said to her clergyman husband, 'How can you still believe in God, now this has happened?' to which he replied: 'Things like this happen to other people every day, and I still believed in God – how can I cease to believe because it has now happened to me?'

Death in a family can unite its members, but it can also lead to division if one member of the family finds it impossible to cope. It can lead to a growing coldness between parent and child.

C.S. Lewis and his brother found themselves cut off from their father during the last illness of their mother:

'For us boys the real bereavement had happened before our mother died... They say that a shared sorrow draws people closer together; I can hardly believe that it often has that effect when those

who share it are of widely different ages... [My father's] nerves had never been of the steadiest and his emotions had always been uncontrolled. Under the pressure of anxiety his temper became incalculable; he spoke wildly and acted unjustly. Thus by a peculiar cruelty of fate, during those months the unfortunate man, had he but known it, was really losing his sons as well as his wife...' [8]

The death of a baby calls for mutual understanding between the mother and the father; if they can help each other through the mourning process, bearing in mind that the time to reach acceptance is likely to be different for each of them, this can give strength to the relationship which will be lasting. Equally, failure in understanding and tolerance may ruin the relationship for life. There are a number of things that can help maintain a strong relationship between grieving parents. These actions and reactions are outlined in the little booklet 'Healing Together: For Couples Whose Baby Dies' by Marcie Lister and Sandra Lovell, and they include:

- Accepting each others' limitations and each others' grieving style

- Avoiding blame

- Patience

- Readiness to talk together and with others

- Not being afraid to ask for help

- Avoiding big decisions (which may only make things worse)

- Holding and caressing each other

- Keeping healthy – *'It's hard to exercise at first, but it's a great grief-reliever ... it's hard to stay depressed when you're physically active. It will also work off anger, let you sleep better, and control your appetite.'* [9]

Siblings

Siblings are too often forgotten when bereaved families are trying to come to terms with the loss of a child. There is sometimes a mistaken belief that children should be protected from knowledge of death, which leads to them being kept apart at times of crisis, and even to lies being told. The mother of a brother and sister in Greece arranged to have presents sent to them every birthday, supposedly by their father in America, in spite of the fact that he had died years before. No one ever told them the truth, and they were left to hear about his death from a child at school.

But children are surprisingly resilient in the face of death, even their own.

One example of such resilience was the reaction of Martin Benson's small brother Hugh to his death. Martin died peacefully in 1878 while a schoolboy at Winchester, and Hugh wrote to another brother: *'I am so glad that Martin is gone to Jesus Christ … He is St. Martin now'*. But the father Edward Benson, who was later to be Archbishop of Canterbury, was shattered, *'and to the end of his life could not understand why Martin had been taken from him.'* [6]

To keep other children apart from the family at a time of death can lead to great misunderstandings. Children feel abandoned, unwanted, and can express their unease by wayward behaviour, making a bad situation worse. They can even 'bargain' for the dead child's possessions: 'May I have Tommy's mobile phone?' which can make them appear callous and greedy. On the other hand, to be given the belongings of a brother and sister can cause immense distress. In his book 'The People of the Lie'[10], M. Scott Peck describes one young boy suffering feelings of guilt and self-loathing when he was given as a Christmas present the gun with which his brother had committed suicide: 'there was but one interpretation open to him: to believe the gun an

94

appropriate message telling him: *"Take your brother's suicide weapon and do likewise. You deserve to die"* [9]

It is best if the truth of a death is told, using concrete terms without a wealth of physiological detail, and without romanticising. To learn that a little brother or sister has gone back to Heaven 'because God loves him' can be a terrible put off: 'suppose God loves me? He might want to take me too!' Marginalising little children when a brother or sister dies can also aggravate feelings of guilt. Many little children are jealous of the new baby, and they may see themselves as somehow being responsible: 'I prayed that God would take him away – and that's what He did.'

Nor is it easy for little children to understand the immutability of death; they insist on believing that the dead person will be coming back some time. Country children with experience of the death of farm animals, and children with pets fare best in this scenario. Children who have taken part in the burial of a pet hamster learn that that particular hamster is no longer alive and will never come back. So also children who have shared in the mourning process, and have perhaps seen the body, will find that easier to grasp and accept than an attempt to exclude them at such a time.

It can be very difficult for parents to talk to their children about their own grief; frequently the parents feel a revulsion against the living survivors, which is distressing and puzzling for children and which may take some time to be resolved – if it ever is. And the reaction of children can be disconcerting. C.S. Lewis describes the barrier he felt had grown up between himself and his stepsons following the death of their mother: *'I cannot talk to the children about her. The moment I try, there appears on their faces neither grief, nor love, nor fear, nor pity, but the most fatal of all non-conductors, embarrassment. They look as if I were committing an indecency... I can't blame them. It's the way boys are...* [8]

The Paediatric Intensive Care Society has issued a document regarding standards for bereavement care for staff working on such units. This informative and helpful document lists the key points of importance in caring for bereaved siblings:

- Children should be told, whatever their age, that their sibling has died

- It is important to help parents include siblings

- Children soon detect distress and concern in their parents

- Be honest with children

- Explaining what is happening can reduce fear and anxiety for children

- Children react differently to death both as individuals and at different developmental stages and ages

- Children tend not to stay with painful emotions for long

- Physical and behavioural problems can occur long after the sibling's death.[11]

Sometimes little children feel that they must themselves fill the gap left by the dead child. One instance of a small child's misunderstanding of his role in bereavement is the confusion of J.M. Barrie, whose brother David died on the eve of his fourteenth birthday when Barrie himself was only six. Rightly or wrongly, he believed that his mother was incapable of living without David; he therefore tried to help her, not just by taking his brother's place, but also as far as possible by *becoming* David, even to the extent of wearing his dead brother's clothes and trying to alter his appearance in order to look like him.

Janet Goodall describes the damage caused by this misconception: *'Because his mother's memory of the dead boy kept him arrested in adolescence, growing up for Barrie came to signify a betrayal – a threat to his efforts to console his mother.'* [6] Barrie's creation Peter Pan, we remember, wouldn't grow up, and lived in the Never Never land, the land of the Lost Boys. (These were children who, as babies, had fallen out of their prams when their nursemaids were looking the other way – so, presumably, children who had died.)

Provision is made in many hospitals for siblings to be accommodated along with the parents when a baby is dying; it can be made possible for the sibling to see the dead child, even touch or stroke him, and little drawings or gifts can be left for the dead baby to keep. The important thing is for other children to feel needed, part of the scene.

There are some organisations that give support to bereaved children. One such is Jeremiah's Journey, which organises regular meetings with parents present where children can talk and play. *'Many of the activities in the Jeremiah's Journey group help children to build bonds with the person they have lost. We help children through play to talk about their loss and thus teach them two important truths: that it is OK to be sad and it is OK to have fun'.*[12] Jeremiah is a very special teddy bear who understands children who grieve; he belongs to Sheila Cassidy.

Even new babies can feel bereaved, as Janet Goodall explains: *'Because they cry so much for other reasons, their distress when someone dies may not be identified. This is especially so when everyone else in the family is coping with bereavement themselves. It can even be viewed as the last straw that the baby is constantly crying "at a time like this".'* [6] In this case it may be comforting if the baby is placed near a garment or scarf that still smells of the person who has gone. And of course, the presence of another person who will satisfy the baby's needs and demands will gradually fill the gap.

It is well documented that a surviving twin may feel the loss of a sibling, and, if never told of the dead twin, may not understand why they feel as they do. A forty-year-old man recalled: 'I always felt there was something missing from my life; that I was searching for something important but didn't know what it was. It was only when she was dying that my mother told me I had had a twin who died at birth – then these feelings seemed to make sense to me. I wish she had told me earlier, when I was a child.'

Adolescents also are frequently forgotten at times of bereavement. It is as though there is indecision as to whether they are adults who can be included in all the practicalities and the heartache, or are still children who must be kept apart. In the end they find themselves ignored by everyone. Sometimes they are counted on to help care for the rest of the family, and this can be a good thing if the adolescents then feel needed and valued, but will only cause resentment if they feel themselves to be exploited.

The experience of Sarah has left bitter memories. Sarah was sixteen when her sister died from cystic fibrosis, followed shortly afterward by the death of her brother from the same disease. Sarah felt entirely left out of everything that happened to her brother and sister: *'I felt like a spare part in my own family because I was shut out of the illness and everything that happened around that. I wish I had been asked if I wanted to know about it… I did want to be part of it, after all, it was my family.'* Sarah was left with memories of exclusion and jealousy; she felt everyone about her was paying so much attention to her dying brother and sister (whom she also loved) that she was totally forgotten. It was not recognised that at the time, even as she was trying to cope with her grief, she was sitting her GCSE exams and also needed support.[13]

By contrast, Joseph felt well supported by friends and family, although he resented the fact that close family they hadn't seen for many years suddenly appeared: 'I was so happy yet annoyed that it took something like this for them to finally come and see us.'

Joseph's brother James was nine years older, but they were very close, sharing a love of music. This was a comfort to Joseph when James took his own life, as he found a way to express his grief: "James loved music as I do, and to this day I say that music has been my biggest guidance… I found great pleasure and satisfaction in writing a song for and about him."

Joseph was fortunate in that during the period of disruption following the death his wishes were consulted. He was given the choice whether or not to go to the Chapel of Rest – he chose not to go and does not regret it.[13]

It seems bizarre, but it is not uncommon for parents to feel emotionally apart from their remaining children, following the death of one child. In 'Dombey and Son', Dickens' description of the relationship between Florence Dombey and her father shows how completely estranged two grieving people, father and daughter, can be:

> *'Against [her father's door], hardly breathing, she would rest her face and head, and press her lips, in the yearning of her*

love. She crouched upon the cold stone floor outside it, every night, to listen even for his breath; and in her one absorbing wish to be allowed to show him some affection, to be a consolation to him, to win him over to the endurance of some tenderness from her, his solitary child, she would have knelt down at his feet, if she had dared, in humble supplication.

No one knew it. No one thought it. The door was ever closed, and he shut up within.'

Grandparents

Grandparents also need to grieve, and their grief is not only for the loss of a grandchild but also for the unhappiness of their bereaved children. Unfortunately, the relationship between couples and grandparents is not always a good one; well-meaning behaviour can often be seen as interference. When there are good feelings and mutual respect, however, grandparents can be a great help at times of bereavement; a previous similar experience can be a great comfort to the bereaved parents; shared sorrow can be a source of healing for everyone. But grandparents can also bear scars. Sadly, only too often they may themselves have suffered the loss of a child, which they have found it hard to come to terms with, and which makes them feel unable to comfort their own children.

> Ethel's daughter had a stillborn baby, but Ethel, who lived a distance away, was burdened by commitments and felt unable to visit her daughter at that time. Her daughter never really recovered, her marriage broke up, and she became deeply depressed. Twenty years after the stillbirth of her grandson, Ethel still feels guilt at what she perceives her failure to support her daughter.

Willing grandparents, proud to be needed, can be invaluable, particularly when it comes to maintaining the routine of the house and family. They are people who 'know the system', who are trusted by the other children, and who are not afraid to witness tears and heartache. Such a group of grandparents, parents and children can become stronger, more loving, more mutually trusting through the death of a small baby, and as the years pass this is one positive aspect of the bereavement which will not be forgotten.

Friends

Many couples recovering from the loss of a baby find the company of friends more valuable than the immediate family, perhaps because they seem less emotionally involved. The parents feel that they can express their grief more freely to friends, without fearing that they might be enhancing an existing personal sorrow. It seems that bereavement can have the effect of strengthening friendship with those who prove sympathetic and sensitive, and the effect of severing friendship with those who keep away and 'don't want to know.'

Some couples speak of the reassurance and comfort they receive from pets, perhaps because the simplicity of animals, continuing with their normal habits of curling up on a lap, or asking for walks, brings with it a feeling of stability. One father, describing how lonely he felt in his bereavement and how difficult he found it to talk to his friends because of their embarrassment, told his dog of his pain. He could pour out all his sorrow, anger and frustration, and his dog could not answer him with words, but was there, listening to him.

Caregivers

'I could lie down like a tired child/And weep away the life of care', said Shelley – and how those who are responsible for the welfare of babies and their parents would agree with him! 'Caring for the caregivers' is described in detail in Chapter 10 of my book 'Pain, Distress and the Newborn Baby.'[4] In the caring professions, there is a chronic shortage of personnel, funding, respect and recognition; and yet most of us love the work we do and remain in our special fields all our working lives. The Third Maternity Services Advisory Committee Report of 1985 states: *'… stress will be exacerbated by a high work load and insufficient staff, and senior staff should watch that high motivation, however commendable, does not lead staff to work grossly in excess of their normal duty.'*[14]

The ambience of the Neonatal Intensive Care Unit plays a large part in the well-being of nurses. Nurses who have the most positive approach work in an atmosphere where a good relationship exists within the team; sporting events, evenings out, enjoyment of mutual interests are popular. Also the opportunity for further education, participation at conferences, and for carrying out research plays a large part in the relief of stress; even if lengthy periods of study leave are not possible, half-day or day release for seminars has been found to help nurses retain their confidence.[4]

The relationship existing between neonatal staff will have an effect on parents and babies. Jaques et al. in 'Parent-Baby Attachment in Premature Infants' said: *'Until they come to terms with their own feelings about the job it may be difficult for nurses and doctors in neonatal units to understand parental attitudes and to cope with parents' feelings.'*[15] The Maternity Services Advisory Committee Report shows that stress between parent and nurse can arise if the nurse, feeling her responsibility, becomes too authoritarian, and shows her anxiety by sharp criticism and reproach. It should be remembered that often the stress of witnessing the long struggle to live of a very fragile infant has a maturing effect on young parents, and the support and approval of the neonatal team will go a long way to reinforcing this maturity.

Stress can be engendered between nurses and doctors, too. An experienced neonatal nurse can easily resent the authority of a junior doctor, himself learning by experience. Consultant paediatricians and neonatologists have heavy responsibilities they cannot share; they are the ones who ultimately confirm life and death decisions, and must confront unhappy and angry parents with bad news. And 'death' is often viewed as a personal failure.

There are stress and counselling services available in some Regional Health Authorities; effective counselling may be supplied by psychotherapist, hospital chaplain, or trained bereavement counsellor. But peer support is essential; all neonatal staff feel grief and regret at the death of a baby, and mutual sharing of grief is always beneficial if only everyone concerned would feel this was possible. The CDCA (Constructive Dialogue for Clinical Accountability) has issued a useful set of guidelines for professional carers: 'Laying the foundations: Caring for Bereaved Families in Hospital' (see appendix 4) and the book 'Relating to Relatives: breaking bad news, communication and support' by Thurstan Brewin with Margaret Sparshott, also gives valuable guidance to those working in the hospital environment and primary care.[16]

Parents, family, friends and carers are all included in the pains of bereavement. As John Bowlby says: *'The loss of a loved person is one of the most intensely painful experiences any human being can suffer. Not only is it painful to experience, but it is also painful to witness, if only because we are so impotent to help.'* [17] None the less, we must do the best we can.

References

1. *Sudden Death – Shattered Lives.* Child Bereavement Charity Conference, London, 13th June 2002.

2. Kimble, D. L. (1991) Neonatal Death: A Descriptive Study of Fathers' Experiences. *Neonatal Network*, **9**, No.8.

3. Hay, B. (1990) *Forgotten fathers?* BLINK (Blisslink Newsletter) **2**, autumn/winter, 1,4.

4. Sparshott, M. (1997) *Pain, Distress and the Newborn Baby.* Blackwell Science, Oxford.

5. McHaffie, H.E. (2001) *Crucial Decisions at the Beginning of Life.* Radcliffe Medical Press Ltd., Abingdon.

6   Goodall, J. (2000) Grieving Parents, Grieving Children. In: *Representations of Childhood Death.* (Eds. Avery, G. & Reynolds, K.), Macmillan Press Ltd., London.

7. Kushner, H.S. (1992) Wh*en Bad Things Happen to Good People.* Pan Books, London.

8. Lewis, C.S. (1955) *Surprised by Joy: The shape of my Early Life.* Fount Paperbacks, HarperCollins Publishers, London.

9. Lister, M. & Lovell, S. (1991) *Healing Together: For Couples Whose Baby Dies.* A Centering Corporation Resource, Omaha, USA.

10. Peck, M.Scott (1990) *People of the Lie: The Hope for Healing Human Evil,* Arrow Books Limited, London.

11. Paediatric Intensive Care Society Report (2002) Standards for Bereavement Care 2002. Obtainable from: Dr. C.G.Stack, Honorary Secretary, PICU, Sheffield

Children's Hospital, Western Bank, Sheffield S10 2TH. Price £10

12.   Jeremiah's   Journey.   www.jeremiah'sjourney.org.uk. info@jeremiahsjourney.org.uk

13.   *Baby and Child Death – Managing the issues.* Child Bereavement Charity Conference, London, 15th May 2001.

14.   Third Maternity Services Advisory Committee Report (1985) *Staffing for Postnatal and Neonatal Care*, 8. p.43-47

15.   Jaques, N.C.S., Hawthorne Amick, J.T. & Richards, M.P.M. (1983) Parents and the support they need. In: *Parent-Baby Attachment in Premature Infants* (eds. J.A Davis, M.P.M. Richards & N.R.C. Roberton) Croom Helm, Beckenham.

16.   Brewin, T. with Sparshott. M, (1996) *Relating to the Relatives: breaking bad news, communication and support*, Radcliff Medical Press ltd. Abingdon, Oxen

17.   Bowlby, J. (1969) *Attachment.* Pelican Books, London

PART III

LIFE AFTER DEATH

'You thought never again could you take an interest in the world and retain friendships and attend weddings and happy occasions of other people's children. You were certain you could never live through the trauma. But you will.

There is no doubt in your mind that you never again could enjoy yourself. Never want to travel. Never give parties – or attend them. Never have fun. You would only be sorrowful and certainly you would never laugh. Above all, not laugh. But you will.

You will do all that and you will do more.'

Harriet Sarnoff-Schiff. (1979) The Bereaved Parent.

CHAPTER SEVEN
WHAT WENT WRONG?

Parents remember the death of a child

'The only people who can teach us about suffering – both for the sake of our own preparations and our attempts to comfort others – are the sufferers themselves.'

Philip Yancey. Where is God When it Hurts?

The Child Bereavement Trust (now known as the Child Bereavement Charity)[1] organises impressive conferences, with an audience representing a broad spectrum of professions connected with the deaths of children: doctors and nurses, midwives, pathologists, health visitors and social workers, police, coroners and coroners' clerks, lawyers, funeral directors, clergy, and journalists. All these concerned people are there to listen, to ask questions, and to learn from each other.

At these conferences much time is devoted to the personal testimonies of families who have lost children under particularly distressing circumstances. Their experiences are varied, but because of their importance as representative of all bereaved parents, and because their witness has so much to teach all the professions present what support bereaved parents need (and what they don't need!) I am devoting this chapter to some of their stories, taken from two of the conferences, in May 2001 and June 2002. There is no need for comment; the stories speak for themselves:

John and Alexa (Real names)

John expressed the anguish he and his wife felt when facing the termination of her pregnancy at 20 weeks gestational age; Benedict had a rare disorder known as 'body stalk defect', and his condition was inoperable. John's experiences with the consultant and other members of the medical team were mainly positive, but he was hurt by the lack of response from the community service after Benedict's death. John emphasised the importance of the words people use and the way things are said; the only person who contacted them was the health visitor, whose opening remark: '*Hello Alexa, I believe you're home from hospital having had a termination for abnormality*' was not guaranteed to comfort. Otherwise, the grieving parents heard nothing – no call, no visit from the doctor or midwife.

John felt that people make judgments following antenatal death, based on age, weight, or the fact of a termination. Access to a baby memorial service was denied because '*Special Care Babies are special because they have lived*'; Benedict was delivered into a metal dish, the place for clinical waste. The only person who seemed to recognise that Benedict was 'their baby' was the undertaker, who stood at the door and said 'I've brought baby Benedict home.' '*That made a lasting impression, because at the end of the day, that's what he was – our baby*'. Alexa found help, and has helped others, by recording her thoughts in a book of poetry: 'Benedict: a child of mine.'

> '*For born in sorrow*
> *In sorrow does he return to me*
> *Comes close and is cherished.*
>
> *Sadness and love woven within*
> *Enrich my tapestry*
> *But the time has come to lift my eyes*
> *And see a new horizon.*
> *So I shall take courage and pack my bag*
> *Fling wide the gate*
> *And step out.*'[2]

Alexa Warden. From the poem 'Take Courage'
in 'Benedict: a child of mine', September 1999

Mark and Nancy

Mark and Nancy are the parents of Lucy, who died in her cot at 4 months. This occurred over twenty years ago, but for Mark and Nancy the death was handled in a sensitive and caring way. Mark was a police constable at that time, so was familiar with the proceedings following any sudden death, but inevitably the suspicion that they might themselves have been responsible for the death of their child was very hurtful and added to their distress. Later, Mark was to work with a cot death trust, and write a leaflet giving guidance to police officers should they be called to attend a cot death.

Mark pointed out that parents themselves do not always agree as to what is the best procedure; Nancy wanted the doctor who arrived after the death to attempt resuscitation – Mark did not feel that this was appropriate; he wanted to protect Nancy and did not suggest she hold Lucy before she was taken from them – Nancy would have loved to have held her daughter one last time, but did not dare say so.

It was only recently that Mark and Nancy discovered that Lucy's brain had been removed at post mortem and had not been returned to them. In spite of this, Mark and Nancy still feel that they have buried Lucy, but they accept that many people might feel differently; this difference in attitude Mark believes creates a terrible dilemma for professionals who might withhold information in order to be protective. Mark is aware that further research is carried out on such samples as and when medical science progresses. '*Without the ability to retain these samples this research cannot be done and therefore in our view the chance of prevention may well be lost.*'

Rebecca and Stephen

Rebecca and Stephen's son Tom died aged nine-and-a-half months, but their grief began at the time of his birth, when oxygen starvation led to severe cerebral palsy. Lack of information contributed largely to their grief: *'poor communication, especially from health professionals, can be even more distressing than the tragedy itself.'* Needing information on the cause of Tom's problems led to litigation – this *'was not about redress – simply a need for information, acknowledgment, and trust.'* Rebecca (who is herself a nurse) suggests seven points for health professionals to consider:

- A culture that is open and safe – where families can ask 'why?' and service providers can say 'sorry'

- A system which **all** staff and service users understand

- Experiential training to increase staff self-awareness of their own experiences of loss and how this influences their work

- An organisation that would invest to train and empower front line staff

- An access point for coordinated information rather than the lottery of 'who you get'

- Enabling families' very different needs to be met – e.g. fundraising, counselling, resolving issues

- A bereavement advisor – someone who is trained to understand loss and grief and can guide families through the range of issues of loss and grief

Maureen

Maureen lost her husband in a family argument when he was stabbed by her brother-in-law. She was left with two children, and she was seven-and-a-half months pregnant at the time. She found that immediately after the death, she almost forgot she was pregnant; the coming baby seemed totally irrelevant. Her husband was dead, and the coming baby seemed unreal.

Maureen's grieving was distorted by the impression given by those investigating the crime that she was herself guilty in some way. She felt that she had never been allowed to grieve properly and come to terms with her loss. She had several comments to make on the way response was made to her needs:

- She was annoyed that it was thought she wouldn't be able to cope – she didn't want to be "treated like a little lamb"

- She felt that no one seemed to recognise that she was a grieving wife – she felt that to the police she was "just another domestic crime"

- She pointed out that everything is magnified when you are grieving – little things assume tremendous importance; for instance, an engaged tone on the telephone feels like a rejection

- She realised her children needed friends, and to know the same violence couldn't happen to them

She had this advice to those who surround the bereaved. *We are all human; try to be who you are. And remember that a loss is a loss – whatever the counselling, still the children have no father.'*

The experiences of the previous families with professional carers were generally of sympathy and regret, in spite of misunderstandings. The experiences of the following two families are very different:

Matthew and Angela

Peter was a preterm baby who suffered a brain haemorrhage when he was four-days-old. This led to hydrocephalus and a series of shunt operations, until he was diagnosed as spastic quadraplegic at two years of age. Peter died of undiagnosed volvulus aged 4 years and 15 days; nobody had listened to the parents: *'they had us down as two paranoid parents making a fuss about nothing, we constantly said that things were getting worse; Peter's cries were ignored until they fell silent.'* The presiding doctor said that mental retardation made it difficult for Matthew to communicate pain and its whereabouts; but the little boy screamed and extended his body violently (behavioural signs of pain which are easy to read). According to Matthew: *'it is important for consultants down to auxiliary nurses to listen to parents when we say our children are taking a turn for the worse, more especially when it is parents of a special needs child. We know our children the best, often when you ask questions you can easily be made to feel as if you are wasting their time.'*

Peter was one of the children caught up in the Alder Hay hospital organ retention scandal. A post-mortem revealed septicaemic shock, acute haemorrhagic infraction of the small bowel, and volvulus, but unbeknownst to his parents, all his organs were taken, as well as heart, brain, glands, bone muscle, and a piece of skin. Matthew feels that since the scandal, they have entered a new cycle of distrust: *'it is a world of patronising arrogance and deceit… someone has stolen and taken away the most precious and sacred things… Peter's first funeral has been made a mockery of…'*

Anna

Anna lost her first baby shortly after birth, following mismanagement of her long labour. She became aware that something was wrong when she saw the staff panicking. She was eventually given a general anaesthetic and woke to find herself in the recovery room, alone – no husband, no nurse, no one. Her husband was in the neonatal unit with their daughter, who was still fighting to live. He was asked if he would give permission for life support to be discontinued. Since he did not at all understand what the problem with his daughter was, he refused. So, while she was still recovering from the anaesthetic, Anna herself was asked to agree that the ventilator breathing for her baby should be switched off. She felt she was not given complete information and was hurried into making a decision she did not fully understand, when all she wanted was to be able to hold her baby, with her husband beside her. She was never given this opportunity.

During the inquest that followed, the medical team was praised and exonerated by the coroner. This made Anna angry, as she felt mistakes had been made and no one was admitting to them. It seemed as though the doctors were mutually congratulating themselves on their treatment; one doctor even seemed as though 'on a soap box.' Midwives who had witnessed the birth were not called to be present at the inquest, and Anna felt that she was herself her baby's only advocate.

The findings of the inquest were reported in the local newspaper – Anna had not been aware there was to be such an article, as no one had asked her for her story. When she complained that the report did not give the true facts, the editor quoted 'the public's right to know', saying that according to him the doctors deserved praise. This all happened three months after her daughter had died, and by this time all both parents wanted was to be allowed to get on with their lives.

Several of the parents at the conference spoke of the persistent intrusion of the press, and how this compounded their distress. They felt that very real tragedies were being turned into a 'media circus', as though death was somehow put on to provide a scoop and sell newspapers. They also felt that they should be informed if stories of their children's death were to appear in the papers. Anna had a message for reporters: *'As soon as you lose humanity, and continue knocking the door even when asked to stop – leave the profession;'* and *'truth would be nice!'* she said.

The experiences of these families, and others, formed the basis for the conferences; again and again, the importance of good communication, empathy, and the essential dissemination of information was emphasised. But it seemed, from the accounts of other speakers, that work is already being undertaken which it is hoped will improve communication between bereaved families and the professions.

A **chief superintendent** from a regional constabulary now organises family liaison training for those who visit the bereaved – fully-trained family liaison officers are assigned to every enquiry. He admitted that one of the problems for the police is the conflict between sympathy with the bereaved and suspicion, since frequently the perpetrator is found to be a member of the family.

A **coroner** quoted the aim of the Charter for his service: *'to provide a caring efficient service making all decisions with respect and dignity for the deceased and compassionate consideration for family, friends, and all with whom we have contact at what will be a most stressful time.'* The coroner believes that everyone attending a court must understand everything that has happened; parents of dead children particularly need to know the how, when and why of a sudden death.

There has been some criticism that student midwives are not introduced to information relevant to the pathology of perinatal loss; on the other hand, care of the bereaved cannot completely be learned from a text book; contact and personal experience are surely the best teachers.

The **bereavement support midwife** saw her role as the support of parents following miscarriage, ectopic pregnancy, stillbirth, neonatal death, and termination of pregnancy. She believes members of staff are inhibited in their relationship with bereaved parents because they are afraid of 'something going wrong.' She feels that professionals should not make assumptions about family needs; families are made up of individuals. It is impossible to remove the pain, but the quality of the mourning experience can be improved. Her advice to professionals is: *'be yourself, give yourself, be honest'*

The interests of a **nursing sister** from an accident and emergency department were predominantly centred on the education and support of staff to ensure they are fit to practise. She also believes that paying attention to the expressed needs of the families and listening to their perception of events will better enable the development of staff training suited to their needs.

A **paediatric pathologist** emphasised the importance of an expert post-mortem, which would give parents answers they desperately need to know and a definite diagnosis that would help to ease feelings of guilt. One of the problems in communication is that pathologists are very often anonymous, shrouded in secrecy. She herself likes to visit bereaved parents and speak to them personally.

A **general practitioner** saw his role of family doctor as *'the rock that is not going to go away.'* He confirmed what many of the parents said, home visiting at a time of bereavement is important: *'Everyone concerned is a human being; it is important for the doctor also to show his human side.'*

The special interests of the **hospital chaplain** were in the spiritual care around pregnancy loss, care of the dying, bereavement, and medical ethics. He, like the others, stressed the importance of listening to what people themselves want: *'Do what is desired by the individual, not what the prayer book says.'*

Evidently, the old days of doctors being perceived as superior and untouchable beings are gone; people would prefer doctors to be human beings, rather than automata. Patients and their relatives see themselves rather as partners, and want to take their share of decision-making. Some participants from the medical profession stressed the importance of 'informed consent'; others thought that 'participation' would be a better word than 'consent', believing that the old 'paternalism' of the medical profession now causes great anger.

There has lately been an increase in public expectations. Obviously there is much to be learned from listening to bereaved families and those who minister to them; we learn from them and from each other. Happily, people are much more aware now of the trials and pitfalls in wait for those who take their professional work too much for granted; the old days of indifferent and impersonal doctors and nurses are gone. Doctors no longer see themselves as God, seated above on an unreachable cloud; nurses no longer see themselves as Florence Nightingale, hidden behind a concealing cap and starched apron. The bereaved need emotional care as well as practical care; there should always be someone accessible, not to impose help but to give help when needed. Professionals are required to be open; parents will never give up until they have found out what they want to know. Mistakes can be forgiven; but arrogance, coldness, and indifference – never!

Children and babies who die belong to themselves and to their parents; lack of respect, failures of communication and insensitivity to the feelings of parents and siblings have caused untold heartache, and have left families with lifelong memories of revulsion and resentment. Too many parents are frustrated by the failure of family, friends and professionals to see the lost child as a person who has existed, even if the death took place before the baby could be born. But, at conferences like those organised by the Child Bereavement Charity, we at last begin to feel the wind of change.

References

1. The Child Bereavement Trust is now known as the Child Bereavement Charity, Aston House, High Street, West Wycombe, High Wycombe, Bucks., HP14 3AG,

    Tel. 01494446648, enquiries@childbereavement.org.uk, www.childbereavement.org.uk

2. Warden, A. (1999) *Benedict: A child of mine.* Poems by Alexa Warden written following the death of her baby. (Obtainable from the Child Bereavemnt Charity, See address above.)

CHAPTER EIGHT
THE DESTINATION OF THE BODY

'Perfect little body, without fault or stain on thee.'

Robert Bridges: On a dead child.

I have just been watching a re-run of the US T.V series 'Quincy' – I like these old reruns which show 'humanity' in humans, and Quincy certainly does that! This particular episode was about a community midwife, trained in Texas but unlicensed in L.A., who was accused of murder when she was (supposedly) guilty of the death of a baby through negligence. Of course (this being fiction) she was innocent and proved so by Dr. Quincy; she was guilty only of tending to a refugee woman who had fallen through the net of 'civil rights' and could not call on the American social services for support. In the same episode, however, no one was accused of murder when another baby died because a hospital refused to admit a woman in labour who did not fit into an acceptable category for insurance. So the crucial theme of this episode was the refusal of officialdom to depart from regulation procedure even in cases of emergency.

This was an interesting and poignant programme for a midwife to watch, and of course it was 'all right in the end' – but was it? What was not shown were the feelings of the parents of the children following the deaths of their babies. Did they give way to anger in face of a system that denied their babies the right to live? Did they say 'goodbye' to hope and forget the dead babies who had never breathed? Or did these deaths leave scars of guilt and anger that would last forever? Since both the fictional cases could really happen, these questions are of paramount importance; there should be concern with the problem of infant death, how it is perceived, and the mutilation it can leave behind if not accepted and absorbed by the bereaved.

'Virtually everything that can be imagined about death has been imagined', says the Dictionary of Religious Belief. The earliest human imagination of death was entirely realistic; since breath returns to air and the body to dust, there is nothing that can survive. Gradually, however, the idea that 'the dead' would somehow reappear in some form became universally accepted; they would resurface in the genealogical family or present themselves in dreams and memories, and they were therefore maintained through ritual. Everyone must die, in order to give way to those who newly come into the world; there is not room for all to live forever. In this way death can be seen as a sort of sacrifice for the living, a 'way of exchange' as Charles Williams describes it. And this acceptance of death as a necessary sacrifice that could not be avoided led to the development of the idea that there might be some form of continuance after death.

We all know that there is decomposition of the body after death, which is why it is important that those we love cannot remain with us, but must be buried, or burnt, or embalmed. But is this all? Is the destination of the body important? To some people, according to their religious beliefs or their instinctive feelings, the destination of the body after death is important; to others this matters not a jot. Whichever it is, the body of a dead child does not belong to a hospital or to a pathologist; it belongs to himself first, and then to his parents, who have to make choices on his behalf, and it behoves those who communicate with parents to be quite clear about what is going to happen.

When a baby dies in hospital it is usual for a request for a post-mortem to be made to the parents, not only in order for a correct diagnosis to be given, but also for the benefit of future sufferers. When I first started to research this book, the newspapers were full of the story of the retention of body parts from dead fetuses, babies and children by some of Britain's largest and most respected hospitals. Bit by bit, the full horror of these stories appeared, and parents were aghast to have organs of their children returned to them piecemeal. To many this meant a regular return to their child's grave, and yet more prayers to be said. Some parents discovered that the body they originally mourned and buried consisted only of skin and bones (and sometimes not all of those); brain, heart and all other organs had been removed without permission, and were being stored in hospital basements for use by pathologists in research, or waiting to be sold to pharmaceutical companies for whatever purpose they deem fit.

Nor was this anything new. In the 1950s, thousands of dead babies were pillaged for their bones, in order for research to be undertaken into the effects of radiation on the human body. These anonymous babies were registered by number, age, date of death, and district – not names – and £1.1s. was paid for each; not to the mothers, of course, they never knew what happened to their dead babies. Body snatching became a public service, and search was made particularly in poor countries and inner cities. Doctors believed they knew best, and it was assumed no one would mind.

I use the word 'horror' for this unlicensed body donation, but the use of organs for beneficial research is in fact not horrible to many. Some parents are only too happy to think that the death of their own child may at least show the way towards cure for another. The word 'horror' is used for the way the very existence of the parents was ignored. Why was there failure to gain permission for such procedures? Why was the meaning and purpose of the post-mortem never explained to parents? Was it because of fear that permission would not be given? Or was it because the doctors were reluctant to consult with parents on such a painful subject at such a time? This, like the preceding chapter, brings up the whole question of 'communication' between doctor and patient/parent.

It has been said that doctors and nurses must of necessity desensitise themselves to their patients' pain in order to do their work; that they must be dispassionate in order to protect themselves against the constant stress caused by grief and death. But although this is to a certain extent true, it is the failure to see their patients and patients' families as complete people, body and soul, mind and feeling, and their inability to empathise with this in light of their own humanity, which sometimes leads them to misunderstand the importance of complete honesty in their dealings. It may seem obvious, even naïve, but surely if the professional person facing the parents would only think: 'What if this was my own child, returned to me as an empty shell, his parts taken and perhaps sold by those to whom he does not belong?' It is the ownership here that is in question; pathologists, researchers, and pharmaceutical companies do not own the bodies of other people's children, living or dead. They do not have an inalienable right to dispose of what does not belong to them.

Frequently, senior doctors have had to speak to parents about the death of a baby, and ask permission for a post-mortem to be performed. Usually permission is given; if it is withheld, this wish is respected. Did the senior doctor always know what happened to the bodies following the post-mortem, or did the pathologist use the organs of the bodies as he thought fit?

I have seen many people die, and personally am convinced that at the moment of death something that is the essence of the person leaves the body behind and moves on. Except in cases of violent or sudden death, I have seen again and again how gradually and quietly, towards the end of life, the person withdraws from his loved ones and his surroundings. Dearest relatives should remember this; such a withdrawal is not a

124

rejection of love, but a relinquishment of all that holds the dying one to life. Leo Tolstoy recognised this, when he described the death of Prince Andrei in 'War and Peace:' *[Princess Marya and Natasha] saw that he was slowly and quietly slipping further and further away from them, and both knew that this must be so, and that it was well…. They did not weep for their personal sorrow; they wept from the emotion and awe that filled their souls before the simple and solemn mystery of death that had been accomplished before their eyes.'*

In Chapter Ten we will see how the different religions consider the treatment of the body of a child after death. To many faithful people the importance of an 'intact body' is essential, if the dying one is not to enter God's kingdom maimed; imagine their horror on learning that all they had been given to bury was an empty shell.

For most parents, the body of the child who has just died is also important to hold and caress; at least then they will be able to take with them some memory of loving actions. Some parents, if the baby dies in hospital, cannot bear to say goodbye; they will return for some days after the death, even asking to have their baby brought up from the morgue. Others, however, can hardly bear to look at their dead child, and hurry away, hoping to forget what has happened. In these cases it is often wise to take some photographs of the dead baby and keep them in a safe place, so that they can be given to the parents later, if they regret their decision.

For Willow and John it was a comfort to them later that they had kept a vigil by their dying child. She died at dusk; they watched over her through the night, then bathed and dressed her in the morning. Then, they felt they could say goodbye to her, and were free to grieve.

There are other ways to lighten the load of bitter memories, which we will see later. The most important thing is to listen to parents' wishes, and keep them informed of all that is taking place; and to grieve with them, too. Often babies who die in hospital have spent many weeks on the neonatal unit, taking their two steps forward to one step back.

I and my colleagues have wept with the parents over the deaths of many babies. We do not repent – it is no shame for doctors and nurses to grieve.

CHAPTER NINE
THE EXISTENCE OF THE SOUL

*'It appears that throughout the world man has been seeking something
beyond his own death, beyond his own problems, something that will be
enduring, true and timeless. He has called it God, he has given it many
names; and most of us believe in something of that kind, without ever
actually experiencing it.'*

Jiddu Krishnamurti: The Awakening of Intelligence.

Many people long to believe that there is existence beyond death;
when so many people experience suffering, hardship, misery in
this life, surely, we say, this cannot be all? A life after death is
seen not so much as a reward but a relief – otherwise, why exist
at all? The basic human instinct for justice forces us to search for
a meaning behind the inequalities of this world. The existence of
a part of ourselves which is not 'body', which will not decay, and
which may progress to a happier destination after death, gives
many humans the strength to persist on striving in a world which
offers periods of unhappiness to most, and limitless suffering to
many. This embodied but spiritual part of ourselves is called the
'soul'.

Atheists do not believe in an immortal soul; they believe
this life and all it contains is all there is and will be. This certainty
can give them great strength when matters of life and death are
considered. They will resist death with all the fighting strength
they have, but essentially death, since it is nothingness, does not
have to be feared – defied maybe, but not feared. Agnostics, on
the other hand, who can believe only in the material world, as all
else is 'unknowable', can fear this unknown when it approaches
them. Agnostic and atheist parents frequently experience total

loss at the death of a child, since not only has there been no promised life, there is also no image, for them, of a celestial future for babies lovingly cradled in the bosom of a parental God.

Collins dictionary gives this definition of the word 'soul': *'the spirit or immaterial part of man, the seat of human personality, intellect, will, and emotions: regarded as an entity that survives the body after death.'* In sacred scripture the term 'soul' also refers to the innermost aspects of man, that which is of greatest value in him, that by which he is most especially in God's image; the soul is therefore spiritual principle in man. Can these spiritualities be attributed to the preborn infant, and if so, at what stage of development can the soul be said to exist? Of course we have no way of knowing, but the great religions have their philosophies, basically very similar to each other. The only great point of difference is the eventual destination of this 'soul'.

Christianity

According to the Catechism of the Catholic Church (366), the soul *'is also immortal: it does not perish when separated from the body at death, and it will be reunited with the body at the final Resurrection.'*[1]

The First Vatican Council took the view that spiritual souls are not 'produced' by the parents, but are created directly by God and infused into the developing embryo. There, the unity of soul and body is seen to be so profound that one has to consider the soul to be the 'form' of the body, soul and body in their union forming a single nature. The Encyclical Letter of Pope John Paul II published in 1995 had this to say: *'In every child which is born and in every person who lives or dies we see the image of God's glory. We celebrate this glory in every human being, a sign of the living God, an icon of Jesus Christ.'*[2]

But also according to Christian belief humanity is innately sinful, as is illustrated by the Old Testament story of the Fall of Adam and Eve and their exile from the Garden of Eden. We, as human beings made in God's image, were given free will by God, but have chosen to be disobedient rather than surrender, and have lost our original purity. Because of our permanent state of imperfection, we cannot save ourselves, but can only hope to be forgiven by our loving Father. But how can we, imperfect as we are, be united to a God who is Perfection? This contradictory state of affairs was resolved by the death of Jesus on the Cross, when he took the sins of humanity into himself. We are not able to save ourselves by good works, but we achieve eternal life through the 'grace' of God.

Judaism

The vision of Judaism originates in the first chapter of the Hebrew Bible, as God says: *'Let us make man in our own image, after our own likeness.'* In the words of Chief Rabbi Jonathan Sacks: *'every human life is sacred and irreplaceable because each of us carries within us a trace of God's presence in the world.'* [3] In Judaism, human life is sacred, and the body is honoured as the instrument through which the soul is manifested in this world. Indeed, some Jewish thinkers believe that body and soul are an indivisible entity.

In Jewish law, personhood begins at the moment in the birth process when the head emerges. Until then a fetus is human life and a *potential* person, but is not an *actual* person. The soul is believed to enter the body at the point of birth, if the baby is born alive. The possibility of life after death was not certain in ancient Judaism, although in the book of Daniel the possibility is mentioned. However, the Talmud developed belief in life after death, and in Jewish tradition the candle is symbolic of the body and soul. The flame is the soul itself, which reaches ever upwards. By lighting a candle and keeping it burning throughout the Shiva period, it is believed that the soul of the departed will be aided on its journey heavenward.

Islam

The holy book of Islam, the Koran (the Qur'an), states that *'surely we are Allah's and to him we shall surely return',* [4] implying that there is life after death. According to the teachings of Islam, the soul is breathed into the fetus when it is 120 days old.

The belief of Islam is that God wills the destiny of each individual soul, and this destiny must be accepted. Both what Allah gives and takes belong to Him, and He has an appointed time for everyone. The Koran states: *'It is Allah who brought you forth from your mother's womb knowing nothing... Wherever it may find itself and however far it may wander, the human soul is at home only in Paradise. Elsewhere it is in exile'* [5]

Sufism is a branch of Islam. Like all Muslims, the Sufis believe in the unity of God but they take this to include *all beings* in God. Sufism is the religion of the heart, and the wisdom of Sufism is seen in the Gathas, which are the teachings Hazrat Inayat Khan gave to his students: 'Sa'di says, *"Every soul is born with a purpose and the light of that purpose is kindled in his heart,"* [6] and this applies not only to human beings, but to all creatures, great and small.

The whole work of the Sufi is to strive towards soul-realisation. For the mystic the physical body is something he can easily dispense with, and to arrive at this realisation is the object of wisdom. When by philosophical understanding of life he begins to realize his soul, then he begins to stand, so to speak, on his own feet; he is then himself, and the body is to him only a cover. *It is true that a whole lifetime is not sufficient for one to become what one wishes to be. Still nothing is impossible, since the soul of man is from the Spirit of God. And if God can do all things, why cannot man do something?*[6]

Hinduism

There is a Hindu motto that says: 'Truth is One, Paths are many.' Hindus have no single prophet or Messiah and no formal creed or central authority. Most Hindus worship God, the Supreme Spirit, through gods and goddesses. Each god or goddess has certain qualities and characters, which together form the One God, Brahman. Brahman created all things, and to Brahman all things will return.

The Soul (the Jiva) is the Self as it is separated from the material body. Eastern religions deny the existence of a permanent death in the belief that the soul is reborn many times before its final release, when it has attained a state of perfection. In its pilgrimage towards perfection, the soul must pass through four recurring stages: life in the visible world, death, life in the invisible worlds, re-birth. In other words, the soul migrates through a series of bodies, proceeding up and down on its journey dependent on virtue. At last, as the soul grows weary and longs for higher, subtler experiences and more expanded life, it will turn away from all the comforts these worlds can offer, and find delight in meditation, worship, and the compassionate helping of those weaker than itself; the soul no longer seeks to gain pleasure, but only to give service to others. In this way the soul will eventually find freedom.

Buddhism

Buddhism is not a theistic religion; there is no creator God to whom one can pray. Buddha is described as *'a human being who attained full Enlightenment through meditation and showed us the path of spiritual awakening and freedom.'* [7] Buddhists do not believe in an eternal, unchanging soul, but they, like the Hindus, also believe in the turning wheel of birth, death and rebirth, the path to perfection that will eventually lead them to escape from the cycle into the peace of Nirvana. When a saintly person dies, he enters a deathless, peaceful, unchanging state that cannot be described – this is the state of Nirvana:

> *'No suffering for him who is free from sorrow*
> *free from the fetters of life*
> *free in everything he does.*
> *He has reached the end of his road.'*
>
> The Dhammapada [8]

Sikhism

Sikhs believe in one personal God who is the creator and source of all being. For the Sikh, everyone has direct communication with God, and a good life of kindness to others and concern for family and society is the way to achieve salvation. They too believe in reincarnation, so do not mourn for long. Their ultimate aim is to lead a perfect life and so avoid reincarnation.

Reincarnation is linked to belief in 'karma', the cycle of reward and punishment for all thoughts and deeds. The belief is that a person's karma can be changed and improved through the grace of God.

In the long run, time is nothing – intention is all. All the religions offer us different forms of this meaning; some deny the value of life on earth, while others seek a reflection of heaven in the here and now. In the earliest Judeo-Christian traditions the belief developed that 'friendship with God' might be continued after the physical body had died; this could come about either through God resurrecting the whole body limb by limb and breath by breath, or by the continuing existence of the immortal soul. This idea reached fulfilment in the resurrection of Jesus, not only in spirit but also in bodily form; so, soul and body were resurrected together.

References:

1. *Catechism of the Roman Catholic Church*, 1994

2. *Evangelium Vitae* (1995)Encyclical letter addressed by the Supreme Pontiff Pope John Paul II. Catholic Truth Society, Publishers to the Holy See, London.

3. Sacks, J. (2001): *Ethical Issues at the Start of Life*. The Samuel Gee Lecture, Royal College of Physicians, London

4. *The Koran/The Holy Qur'an*: 4:87 (1974) Translated by Dawood, N. J. Revised Edition, Penguin Classics, Harmondsworth, Middlesex.

5. Eaton, Gai (1994) *Islam and the Destiny of Man*. The Islamic Text Society, Cambridge.

6. Khan, Hazrat Inayat (2000): *The Wisdom of Sufism – Sacred Readings from the Gathas*. Element Books Ltd, Shaftsbury, Dorset.

7. Fisher, M.P. (1997): *Living Religions*. I.B Tauris and Co. Ltd., London.

8. *The Dhammapada*. Translated by P. Lal. Farrar, Straus, & Giroux, New York.

CHAPTER TEN
HOLY INNOCENTS

The Paradox

Our death implicit in our birth,
We cease, or cannot be:
And know when we are laid in earth
We perish utterly.
And equally the spirit knows
The indomitable sense
Of immortality, which goes
Against all evidence,
See faith alone, whose hand unlocks
All mystery at a touch,
Embrace the awful Paradox
Nor wonder overmuch.

Ruth Pitter

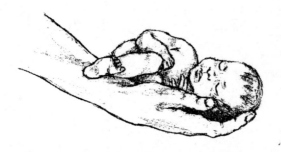

Ruth Pitter's poem 'The Paradox' asks us 'not to wonder overmuch' when confronted with the possibility of an afterlife; we are asked to make the confrontation by faith alone. But how difficult this is for the parents of a baby who has died without first travelling through life! They are bound to wonder what this baby takes with him into that invisible, intangible, and silent place from which he has hardly come. Is he born with a soul, and is this untouched soul returned to eternal life? How important to anyone other than his parents, indeed, is the life of a newborn baby, let alone his death, before he arrives at conscious recognition of the world about him? The world's great religions, in spite of containing within themselves many different interpretations of their basic faith, reflect the most loving and compassionate as well as the most forbidding and judgmental aspects of human nature when they tell us how they value the devotional care of newborn babies.

CHRISTIANITY

Can a newborn baby, who dies before he realises that he has lived, find salvation and reunion with the God who created him for such a short life?

In this chapter, the beliefs of Christians will be briefly discussed under the four categories of Roman Catholic, Orthodox, Anglican, and Non-conformist/Protestant. Life after death forms a central part of their doctrine, with belief and faith in the redemptive powers of Jesus Christ a prerequisite for salvation.

Baptism

The sacrament of Baptism or Christening commemorates the baptism of Christ by John the Baptist, and is seen as the beginning of an individual's relationship with God, through life in his Church. Baptism is a form of purification which is seen to help remove the contamination that is born in humanity – the state of 'original sin' – but it is only through God's compassionate grace that we can be delivered and attain at our death a divine state of being without sin. In some churches baptism takes place only when an individual is old enough to understand the commitment he is making. Some churches baptise infants on the basis of the faith and commitment of the parents, and godparents may be chosen whose role is to help with the spiritual education of the child.

Emergency baptism may be offered a very sick or tiny baby. If there is not time to send for the appropriate priest, anyone may baptise a baby; but preferably it should be someone who has herself or himself been baptised. The following words should be spoken: … '(the child's name), I baptise you in the name of the Father, the Son, and the Holy Spirit, Amen.' At the same time a little water should be sprinkled on the child's forehead.

Baptism has always held great significance for Christians. There was a time, not so many years ago and even in some countries up to this century, when folklore and legend recounted stories concerning the fate of unbaptised babies, many traditions holding that the ghosts of unbaptised babies would remain near the place where they died, clamouring to be released, and never ceasing to haunt their parents or local priests until they had been blessed and committed to the earth. Even now for many parents, even if they are infrequent churchgoers, baptism of a dying baby is of tremendous importance, and failure to perform this ceremony can leave anxiety and heartache; it makes a difference for the baby to be given a name, because a name signifies identity. Nonetheless, this should not be taken for granted; parents should always be consulted before the decision to baptise is taken. If a baby dies unbaptised or is stillborn, a chaplain may offer a naming and blessing ceremony after the death.

Salvation and grace

According to Saint Ambrose, God did not decree death from the beginning, he prescribed it as a remedy: *'Death is, then, no cause for mourning, for it is the cause of man's salvation.'* Attainment of **eternal life** is the goal that governs life, this being characterised by a state of oneness with God. Since Christians are redeemed through the crucifixion of Jesus who takes the sin of the world on himself by his death, salvation is not dependent on good deeds, but comes through the grace of God.

In his encyclical letter of November 2007 'Spe Salvi', Pope Benedict describes eternity as a *'plunging into the ocean of infinite love, a moment in which time – the before and after – no longer exists.'*[1] **Purgatory** is the place where human souls, who did not learn love in this life, could learn it and be perfected in it before they come before the face of God. **Limbo** – a region on the border of hell where it was imagined pre-Christians were confined – was said to be 'the complete natural happiness and joy' for those who have died unbaptised. But although some Christians still maintain it exists, limbo is a theological speculation, and its existence is not officially taught by the Church; the belief has now generally fallen out of favour, and is no longer upheld.

Baptism

According to the Catechism of the Catholic Church published in 1994, children are born with a fallen human nature and so are tainted by original sin.[2] They therefore need baptism to free them from the power of darkness and bring them into the realm of freedom of the children of God, to which all men are called. Baptism, the sacrament of regeneration through water and the Word, is an essential rite for the children of Catholic parents, and preferably should be performed by a priest.

Traditionally, babies were baptised soon after birth, since it was believed that unbaptised children could not achieve eternal life; they would go to limbo. But now children who die without baptism are not condemned: *'Indeed, the great mercy of God who desires all men should be saved, and Jesus' tenderness towards children, which caused him to say: "Let the children come to me, do not hinder them", allows us to hope that there is a way of salvation for children who have died without Baptism.'* [2]

On the same subject, Father Peter Knott in his little book 'Safe in God's Hands' has this to say: *'Since scripture supports belief that God mercifully opens heaven to the unbaptised patriarchs of the Old Testament and to unbaptised martyrs, as in the Feast of the Holy Innocents, we can assume that heaven is not closed to unbaptised babies. If, as we believe, God desires to save all people there must be a chance of salvation for each one even when sacramental baptism is not available.'* [3]

Death is seen as the will of God, and even when mourning one should be happy for the person who has died. If parents are in doubt as to the ultimate destination of their dead child, however, it is hard to see how they can achieve happiness for him. For Christian parents, baptism gives this reassurance. Parents distressed if their baby has not been baptised may find comfort in a funeral service, since these can be held for babies who die. There is no specific funeral service for miscarriage, but some priests will conduct a funeral service for late miscarriages.

Abortion

Catholics believe the souls of their loved ones live on in eternal bliss. Life, however, is always to be respected, and this respect extends to the life and integrity of the human embryo. As to abortion, the official stance of the Roman Catholic Church is to regard termination of pregnancy as murder, and therefore a mortal sin. A baby is considered to have a soul and full human rights from the moment of conception, so: *'since it must be treated from conception as a person, the embryo must be defended in its integrity, cared for, and healed, as far as possible, like any other human being.'*

Pope John Paul II had no doubts as to the moral gravity of procured abortion: *The one eliminated is a human being at the very beginning of life. No one more absolutely* **innocent** *could be imagined… He or she is* **weak***, defenceless, even to the point of lacking that minimal form of defence consisting in the poignant power of a newborn baby's cries and tears. The unborn child is* **totally entrusted** *to the protection and care of the woman carrying him or her in the womb.'* 4

Nevertheless, some Catholic women will seek to obtain a termination if the baby is known to have a serious congenital abnormality, if they risk being a single parent, or following rape. Professionals caring for such women should remember that strict confidentiality is extremely important in these cases, and it should also be remembered that, like many other women of other faiths, Catholic women may later be troubled by permanent and profound feelings of guilt. Normally, priests can give sacrament following confession for an abortion, but there can be exceptions. The Code of Canon Law and Commentary states: *'All involved in the deliberate and successful effort to eject a non-viable fetus from the mother's womb incur 'ipso facto' excommunication'.*5 It is unlikely to come to that, although the woman might need a special dispensation from the 'sin' of abortion.

Pope John Paul II in his encyclical letter acknowledged that in many cases women make a painful and even shattering decision. *The wound in your heart may not yet have healed … Try to understand what happened and face it honestly …The Father of mercies is ready to give you his forgiveness and his peace in the Sacrament of Reconciliation. You will come to understand that nothing is definitively lost.'*

4 And in his letter of November 2007, Pope Benedict wrote: *'God is justice and creates justice. This is our consolation and our hope. And in his justice is also Grace.'* [1]

Eastern Orthodoxy

Salvation and grace

Orthodoxy is the religion of Russia, Greece, and many of the Eastern European countries. Eastern churches generally place more emphasis on the ability of humanity to break out of its earthly bonds and rise into the light, than on the heaviness and darkness of sin. Children born into the Orthodox faith are not only baptised, but are also confirmed and given communion in infancy. Baptism of an infant before he is able to comprehend what that means shows that God loves and accepts his creatures from the moment of birth, even before they can individually come to know and love Him. According to Orthodox belief nothing shows the nature of God's grace more than infant baptism, and the whole emphasis of baptism is not on what the baby does, nor the parents and godparents, but on what God does.

Baptism

Holy Baptism is the first of seven Sacraments in the Orthodox Christian Church. Baptism signifies a mystical burial and resurrection with Christ, so sacramental symbolism requires immersion (burial) of the whole body in the waters of Baptism, and a rising (resurrection) out of them once more. *From the moment the child is received into the Church emphasis is placed on his individuality. He is given his own particular name by which he will be distinguished from every other child of God; this new name expresses also the new life received in Christ through baptism'.* [6]

Baptism is also the sacrament of entrance into light; it opens the eyes of the soul to see Christ, the light of the world. In the early Church, and still sometimes today, the baptismal candle was kept by the one baptised and brought into the church for major events in the person's life. At the approach of death the candle was again lighted for the departure of the soul, thus becoming a symbol of the perseverance of the baptised soul until the return of Christ.

A priest usually performs baptism, but any man or woman can perform it, providing they are Christian and have been themselves baptised. After baptism, an Orthodox child is 'chrismated' (or confirmed) by which means he receives the gift of the Spirit. As soon as possible after this, the child is brought to Communion. He need not wait until he is five or six years' old, as in the Catholic Church – communion is something from which he has never been excluded.

While living in Greece and working on a Greek premature baby unit, I baptised many preterm babies, and was much intrigued by the practice of the Orthodox priests, when undertaking a baptism, of spattering Holy Water over the top of the incubator, thereby baptising the incubator! This was, however, their only solution, since to avoid the ever-present risk of infection they were not allowed to touch the babies themselves – and in any case a total immersion would have been most dangerous!

Theologians believe the soul enters the body at the moment of conception – the 'reason-endowed soul'. Orthodox theologians reject the idea of 'original sin'. Men are thought to inherit Adam's corruption and mortality, but not his guilt. Therefore Orthodox Christians do not believe that unbaptised babies, tainted by original sin, are consigned to oblivion. In spite of this, Orthodox parents of sick babies are usually extremely anxious for them to be baptised and given a name – once again, we see, a name gives identity to the baby.

> It is unwise to assume this, however. A young Greek policeman was furious that his premature baby had been baptised before death, since it meant that he would have to pay for a funeral. He carried the baby away in a shoebox and buried her beside the Isthmus road which runs between Athens and Corinth, where she was later discovered. For this crime, he was duly punished. Since neither parent was allowed to visit the child in hospital no one knew what his wife thought about it all, but it is doubtful if she was consulted before he disposed of her baby in this way.

Anglicanism, Non-conformism, Protestantism

Anglicanism varies considerably in the emphasis given to different parts of Biblical teaching, with High Church Anglicanism being very similar to Roman Catholicism and the lower Church tending towards the less ritualistic approach of non-conformist churches. Both Anglicans and Non-conformists believe that God accompanies a person in life and in death, and for those that love God eternal life in heaven is fairly certain. Both churches place great emphasis on the mercy of God; not all regard baptism as essential in order to enter his kingdom.

Salvation and grace

Methodists follow the teaching of John Wesley and believe in both original sin and total depravity, but cannot accept a depravity so total that it deprives the human will of the power to choose or reject God. They believe that repentance and faith are our contribution to salvation, and they emphasise free will in the question of redemption.

This could suggest that infants, who are born in original sin and have made no such choice, are not capable of redemption because they are not free to will or choose anything. But Methodists also believe that it is not only through their own actions that humans can be saved; salvation can also be given through grace, which is not man's activity but God's.

Baptism

Baptists and other Protestant groups consider baptism appropriate only for adults, since *'a baby cannot make conscious repentance of sin and conversion of heart'*, implied in the ceremony. Children must be old enough to understand and assent to the sacrament. Denominations that do practice infant baptism include **Episcopalians**, **Presbyterians** and **Lutherans**. To **Pentecostal** churches, baptism is very important but here again there is no infant baptism; prayers of thanksgiving may be offered for the newborn baby's well-being, and Pentecostals will gather round the bedside of a sick child to pray and sing hymns. Many churches have a dedication ceremony to welcome infants into the faith community, when parents and the congregation pray for the baby and promise to teach the child the Christian faith. In cases of stillbirth and neonatal death, it is not necessary for a baby to have been baptised in order for a funeral to be held.

Calvinism takes its name from the sixteenth century French reformer John Calvin, who spent the latter part of his life in Geneva. Calvinists also believe that man is born in sin and is corrupted by sin in every facet of his being (total depravity) and is therefore incapable of doing anything to bring about his own salvation. But they too believe humans are the recipients of

God's grace, and therefore infants can be recipients of that grace, which has no basis in any human merit or accomplishment. *The infant, therefore, though incapable of "works" of any kind, may be a subject of Grace – may be operated upon by the influence of the Holy Spirit… and may be adopted into the family of God, even as it is adopted into a human family.'* [7]

Abortion

Many, but not all, Anglicans disapprove of abortion. Termination may be acceptable if the baby has a life-threatening abnormality, or in the case of incest or rape.

In Christianity, as in other religions, there are differences in interpretation of the Scriptures, many of which lead to practices which create tragic dilemmas. The T.V. drama *Kavanagh Q.C.* explored with great sensitivity one of the differences which led to a heartbreaking impasse. This was the refusal by a mother who was a devout member of the Jehovah's Witnesses to allow her critically ill thirteen-year-old son to have a blood transfusion, which would have saved his life. The boy himself also refused this treatment, and when transfusion was forced upon him by law, begged for baptism in order to be cleansed from what he saw as a violation equivalent to rape. The boy eventually died from a haemorrhage, but he was quite aware of the decision he was making, and the mother, though mourning her son, was convinced of the rightness of following what she believed was God's will.

Whether one has such a belief or not, her decision was worthy of respect. Jehovah's Witnesses are devout people who believe that to ingest blood is forbidden by God, and to do so will imperil their immortal soul. How can one not respect these people, who for their faith put themselves through so much pain? But a thirteen year old child has some consciousness of choice; a new born baby has no such choice, and it is this which makes it almost impossible for patient and carer to see each other's point of view. Sympathise, yes – condone, no.

Another example of the abyss between love and belief was the case of a couple whom I encountered while working as a neonatal nurse in Geneva:

> Josette was a member of a sect, whose diet was strictly vegan. When she delivered her baby, she was already malnourished and anaemic and could not produce nearly enough milk to benefit her baby, who became seriously undernourished. Nurses and Doctors persuaded to no avail, both she and her husband were adamant that their child should receive no milk supplement. Eventually, the baby was so distressed and underweight that Josette's will began to weaken (or strengthen!) and she begged to be able to supplement her child's feed, especially as by this time through anxiety and malnourishment her own milk had virtually disappeared. No less a person than the leader of the sect arrived at the unit and threatened the mother with exclusion from the sect if she disobeyed their strict laws. At this time the father placed himself well in the background and held his peace. Josette was in great distress, but she maintained her resistance and the baby was fed and duly thrived.

What happened to the family afterwards I do not know, but Josette's agony as she tried to choose between her baby and her faith was hard to witness; we supported her as best we could while putting the facts before her, but refraining from criticism of the sect to which she was at the outset attached – about that we remained silent.

JUDAISM

Life after death

Jews believe that there is only one God for all the people of the world, whether they believe in him or not. The possibility of life after death is an uncertain feature in their teachings and many Jews rely on the justice of God's ways as to whether or not it exists. If it does exist, it is not a reward for the conduct of life on earth. Jews do not believe in the concept of 'original sin'.

For the first forty days of pregnancy the embryo is considered as 'mere water'. From forty days gestation the fetus is recognised but is not considered to be a full life; it is seen as an extension of the mother, like a limb. In this context it is significant to note that many mothers do in fact see the loss of a baby before or at birth as a 'mutilation'; 'it was as if they ripped a piece of my guts out,' was one mother's description of her feelings.

Rituals and ceremonies

A baby is deemed in Jewish law to have full human rights immediately after birth. For both boys and girls, certain ritual ceremonies are held eight days after the birth of the baby; these include blessings, prayers, songs, and a naming ceremony. However, a baby who has not lived for thirty days is not legally regarded as a fully viable human being, so it is not obligatory for the full traditional mourning rituals to be followed. As a result, although a baby who is miscarried, stillborn, or dies within thirty days is buried in the normal way, the parents may not have all the other rituals and traditions surrounding death to support them. Parents may be distressed by this, especially as there are sometimes misunderstandings if they do not realise that the choice is theirs, and in the next chapter 'Moving On' we will see how lack of sensitivity on the part of individual religious leaders of all the faiths can leave bitter resentment.

Abortion

Although the fetus is not yet considered a person he is, however, human life and a potential person, and as such must be respected. **Termination** therefore is not acceptable for Orthodox Jews as all human life is considered of infinite value; however, in cases of rape, or where the mother's life is at risk, termination may be considered. Peggy Orenstein, in her article, 'Mourning my Miscarriage' has this to say about Western civilisation and its approach to abortion:

> 'There's little acknowledgement in Western culture of miscarriage, no ritual to cleanse the grief. ... Judaism, despite its meticulous attention to the details of daily life, has traditionally been silent on pregnancy loss – on most matters of pregnancy and childbirth, in fact. (At the urging of female rabbis, the Conservative movement ... has, for the first time, included prayers to mark miscarriage and some abortions in the most recent rabbis' manual.) Christianity, too, has largely ignored miscarriage. [8]

Peggy's experiences in Japan will be discussed later in this chapter, under 'Buddhism'.

ISLAM

*'**The holy book of Islam**, the Qur'an, states that 'surely we are Allah's and to him we will return', implying that there is life after death. A newborn baby, then, having no conscience of self is born in innocence; a baby who dies then returns to the God from whom he has just parted.'*

Hadith. IQRA Trust.

Life after death

Islam does not see Man as born into a state of original sin, as do many Christians; for the Muslim, man is born perfect as he has been created by God, and it is in his travels through life that he sins. The Koran addresses the newborn: *'And Allah has brought you forth from the wombs of your mothers – you did not know anything – and He gave you hearing and sight and hearts that you may give thanks.'* [9]

According to the teachings of Islam, children are born pure, and so if they die they are assured of eternal bliss. The death of children is seen as both a trial and a blessing. Islam recognises this and treats the event as such. The bereaved parents are consoled and reminded that the loss – like others – is a trial by which Allah tries even believers. They are further assured that deceased children are going to Paradise, as Allah has promised not to punish any person or people until they have received his Message. Children who have not attained the age of discretion and therefore the age of legal responsibility are obviously not accountable. This would include even the children of unbelievers: *The Prophet Muhammad (praise be unto him) related a vision in which he saw 'children of all people' around Prophet Ibrahim (praise be unto him) in Paradise. Asked if the children of polytheists were also there, the Prophet answered, "Yes, the children of polytheists also."* [10]

The growing child in the womb is respected. The Koran describes the fetus as being created by Allah from an essence of clay, then placed, a living germ, in a safe enclosure. During pregnancy, very great care must be taken of a woman, as it is believed that any unkind word spoken to her will reach the depth of her being, and so resonate in the soul of the child. If she is made to feel bitter or angry then this can create bitterness or anger in the child. Modern studies have shown this to be true; what is known as 'life stress' in a woman can indeed have an effect on her unborn baby.

Many believe that at birth the newborn baby 'listens to the call of prayer', which is manifested by whispering the Declaration of Faith into the baby's ear: 'There is no deity save God, and Muhammed is his messenger.'

Rituals and ceremonies

Every child dies in the true faith. Stillbirth and neonatal death may be completely accepted as 'the will of Allah' or may lead to the suppression of grief, as, since the death was Allah's will, open mourning is not permitted; however, following the death of a child many Muslims demonstrate their sorrow with great emotion. According to Muslim tradition, a baby who dies at or just after birth must be given a name. The body is washed and shrouded and the janazah (funeral) prayer is performed on it and it is buried; the body must be buried in its entirety, nothing should be removed. There is no need for ritual washing for a stillborn baby, nor is a formal religious ceremony required.

When a child dies, no matter how young, even if an infant who has only lived for a few minutes or seconds – so long as he was born alive – the dead body is treated like that of an adult. The only difference is in the kind of supplication made for him in the course of the prayer. While in the case of the adult the congregations seek Allah's pardon for his sins, the supplication over the dead body of a child is: 'O *Allah, make him/her a cause of recompense for us and mercy in the life to come, and as one going before us and a treasure and a reward.*' [11]

Abortion

Concerning termination of pregnancy, Muslims are told in the Koran: *'Lost indeed are those who, in their folly, kill their children… They have indeed gone astray and are not on the right path.'* [12] However, where the mother's life is in danger and the only way to save her is to abort the baby, it becomes necessary to do so, especially before **ensoulment**, at 120 days post-conception. Termination for any other reason is strongly discouraged after ensoulment has occurred.

HINDUISM

Life after death

Hindus believe in the cycle of birth-death-rebirth – they are reborn according to their behaviour in the last life and this may not necessarily be as a human. Parents, wives, husbands and teachers are particularly revered and all forms of life are respected, including the unborn child.

Interestingly, according to traditional Hindu belief the soul enters the body of the baby during the seventh month of pregnancy; it is now known that this is the time when the development of the central nervous system begins to link with the cerebral cortex, the area of the brain associated with attention, learning and behaviour, and the sensation of pain. If a miscarriage occurs before this time there are no special traditional requirements, though individual families may have their own wishes. After seven months the baby should normally be given a proper religious funeral. Mourning for a dead child only lasts for ten days, as after this the soul is believed to be back in the life cycle.

Rituals and ceremonies

During the third or fourth month of pregnancy a *samskar* (or scripture based rite) called *Punsavana* is performed for the protection of the fetus, but the baby is not named until the samskar of *Namakarana*, which takes place between 10th and 41st days of life. This ceremony marks the child's formal entry into the family's sect of Hinduism. He is then given a name according to astrology, after consultation with the Guru.

Stillborn babies, babies and young children are usually buried rather than cremated. Some families may prefer to wash and prepare the baby's body themselves. Even if the baby dies in hospital, parents may also wish for a religious ceremony to take place before the burial. Burial should take place as soon as possible. Traditionally, women do not attend funerals, and this rule can cause heartache. Post-mortems are not forbidden, but many will find the idea abhorrent and distasteful; for some it is important that the body be returned to them intact.

In some Hindu families the stigma traditionally attached to pregnancy loss may still be important. A woman who has had one or more miscarriage, stillbirth, or neonatal death may sometimes be regarded as carrying bad luck and may not be welcome at traditional women's ceremonies surrounding such events as weddings and the celebration of a pregnancy; because of this tradition women can be caused profound suffering through no fault of their own.

BUDDHISM

Life after death

There is a legend that one day a woman went to Buddha, weeping, begging him to restore her dead child to life. Buddha said to her, "Go and bring me a mustard seed from every house where no-one has died." Of course this proved to be impossible, and after a time the woman realised that no household has ever been able to avoid death. She went away to grieve, finally understanding that her child would never come back to her, to live again in the same body. The baby may be lost to the sad mother, but he is not lost in eternity; when a baby dies, since he has had no experience of his present life and has made no decision on how it should be lived, he will return again to the same position in the cycle of life and death.

Rituals and ceremonies/abortion

Japanese Buddhists believed that the existence of a being flowed into it slowly, like liquid; children solidify gradually over time, and were not considered to be fully in the world until they reached the age of seven. In Tokyo, there is a Buddhist temple where dozens of small statues of infants, each wearing a red crocheted cap and a red cloth bib, each with a brightly coloured pinwheel spinning in the breeze, line a shady path. They are the offerings to Jizo, a bodhisattva (or enlightened being) who watches over miscarried and aborted fetuses. In Japanese the word for a miscarried fetus is **mizuko**, which means 'water child'.

It was expected that the Jizo would help the mizuko to find another pathway into being. The little statues and the gifts bereaved parents bring to the temple are intended to wish the lost children well in their new life, when they return to the cycle of life and death.

Sometimes couples perform mizuko kuyo together. Peggy Orenstein, who visited such a shrine, shortly after a miscarriage, quotes William R. LaFleur, author of 'Liquid Life: Abortion and Buddhism in Japan' as saying that *'if they already have children they may bring them along to honor* [sic] *what is considered, in some sense, a departed sibling: the occasion becomes as much a reunion as a time to grieve.* [8] Peggy Orenstein gives a clear account of her own experiences; she was puzzled by the Japanese Buddhists' s seeming acceptance of abortion, while at the same time acknowledging the loss of a human life.: *'Mizuko kuyo contains elements that would satisfy and disturb Westerners on either side of the abortion debate; there is public recognition and spiritual acknowledgement that a potential life has been lost, remorse is expressed, yet there is no shame over having performed the act …The Japanese tend to accept both the existence of abortion and the idea that mizuko is a form of life. I wondered how they could reconcile what seems to me such mutually exclusive viewpoints. But maybe that's the wrong question. Maybe I should wonder why we can't.'* [8]

SIKHISM

Sikhism takes its name from the Fifteenth Century teacher Guru Nanak; the Sikhs were 'disciples, students, seekers of truth.' Some of their beliefs have been understood as a synthesis of the Hindu and Muslim traditions of Northern India, but according to Mary Pat Fisher's book 'Living Religions', Sikhism *'has its own unique quality of independent revelation and history.'* Asked whether he followed the Hindu or Muslim path, Guru Nanak replied: *'There is neither Hindu nor Mussulman, so whose path shall I follow? I shall follow God's path.'* [13] Sikhism emphasises three central teachings as the straight path to God: working hard in society to earn one's own honest living, sharing from one's earnings with those who are needy, and remembering God at all times as the only Doer, the only Giver.

Life after death

A Sikh paediatrician gave me this account of the birth of the soul:

The Soul transcends life, and returns on its pilgrimage to perfection until it can be mature enough to rejoin the Great Spirit who conceived it at the beginning of Time. The Astral Body waits in Infinity for a suitable place of re-entry into the cosmos. Then, when a baby is due to be born, there is a flash in Infinity, a spark, as the Astral Body reignites, and the Soul re-enters the world.

The Soul is born at about 20 weeks' gestational age. At this time, the pre-born infant knows no earthly love but only the love of God. This love fills its being, and it sings praises and cries continually the name of God from within the womb. If at this time the child should die, this love, which is uncontaminated by worldly desire, would take it back to the source of Love, which is God. There it would once again, as an Astral Body, wait for its next suitable and appropriate entry into the world, where it would once again take its place on the turning wheel – turning forward or back according to its choice.

Rituals and ceremonies/abortion

There are no specific religious ceremonies following the death of a Sikh. Traditionally, termination of pregnancy is regarded by many Sikhs with disapproval, but not by everyone. Stillborn babies are usually buried, rather than cremated as are adults. Post-mortems are disliked, but are not strictly forbidden.

All the great religions, as well as pagans, recognise the importance of giving a baby a name; it is this which seems to identify the baby as a person and an individual. In fact, in all the religions respect is shown to the pregnant mother and her baby. Strange, then, that in these modern times, respect is not always shown to either. How has this come about? Perhaps part of the problem is that people working in a clinical setting become fixed on the meaning and importance of their own work and interest, and no longer see the human condition behind their subject matter. Another problem could be that friends and relatives of bereaved parents can be blinded by the 'business of life', and have lost contact with life's basic domesticity. It is easy for us to 'do our own thing' in order to keep up with the speed of day to day living. But grieving for loved ones is not a speedy process.

It seems that most people, whatever religion they profess, believe that if there is such a thing as a happy afterlife, babies who die at or before birth are sure of a place there; how not, since they are not the practitioners but the helpless victims of 'original sin'? None of the great world religions abandon the helpless and innocent. *'The Lord is good to all,'* says the Psalmist, *'and his compassion is over all that he has made.'*

No loving mother could contemplate the thought of her dead child disappearing into nothingness, as though he had never existed. The child she carried and nurtured inside her, and finally lost before she could even show her love, must surely have kept some trace of the creature it was, and promised to be. It is inhuman to consign babies, who have no freedom of will and who have neither been born nor lived to sin, to some Gehenna of flame and darkness. And if humans cannot tolerate such a thought, how could a loving and merciful God?

'For you love all things that exist, and detest none of the things that you have made; for you would not have made anything if you had hated it… You spare all: for they are yours, O Lord, lover of souls.' (Wisdom of Solomon)

References:

1. *Encyclical letter of Pope Benedict (November 2007)*, The Vatican, Rome.

2. *Catechism of the Roman Catholic Church*, 1994.

3. Knott, Fr. Peter. S.J. (1989) *Safe in God's Hands: Healing the hurt of losing your baby.* Incorporated Catholic Truth Society, London.

4. *Evangelium Vitae* (1995): Encyclical letter addressed by the Supreme Pontiff Pope John Paul II. Catholic Truth Society, Publishers to the Holy See, London.

5. The Code of Canon Law and Commentary (1990) Paulist Press International, USA.

6. *Orthodox Baptism.* Copyright: 2002 Starlite USA Productions www.greekamericandjs.com/Baptisi.html

7. Webb, R.A. (1907) *The Theology of Infant Salvation.* Presbyterian Committee of Publications, Richmond, VA.

8. Orenstein, P. (2002) *Mourning My Miscarriage*, The New York Times Magazine, April 21.

9. *The Koran,* 16:78, Penguin Classics, Penguin Books ltd., Harmondsworth, Middlesex.

10. *Hadith* (saying of the prophet Mohammed, recorded by Al-Bakhari)

11. Eaton, Gai (1994) *Islam and the Destiny of Man.* The Islamic Text Society, Cambrige.

12. *The Koran,* 6:140

13. Fisher, M.P. (1997): *Living Religions.* I.B Tauris and Co. Ltd., London.

CHAPTER ELEVEN
MOVING ON

"I don't know when it happened, but at some point I realized that thinking of the baby was no longer accompanied by that searing pain, or that dreadful weight, or that grape-fruit sized lump in my throat. I began to smile inside when I thought of her, happy in the knowledge of her eternal existence and the awareness that she is forever a part of my heart."

Christine O'Keeffe Lafser.
From: An Empty Cradle, A Full Heart.

Memories are all we have left after bereavement. It cannot be overstated how important it is that those recovering from the loss of a child should not be left with bitter memories that may haunt them for the rest of their lives! Such memories can sour relationships within families, sow mistrust between people and medical professionals, blight a happy life with lifelong morbid fancies, and create permanent disunion for those who believe in a loving God. How are these things to be avoided?

There will come a time, sooner or later, when the anguish of grief following the death of a baby begins to ease and life will begin to pick up its natural rhythm again. But grief is a roller-coaster no one can control; the bereft parents can't say to themselves 'Now I am moving on to the next stage', they will be ready to move on when they are ready, not before – and that is as it should be. Pushing grief down too soon will leave bereaved people unsatisfied, aware of incompleteness. Endless grief will damage their own lives and the lives of those about them.

If one or even both parents become fixed in the mourning process, unable to release the dead child, everyone close, partner, other children, family and friends, will suffer for this, and justified resentments will form; justified, because the living have needs which will not be met in this scenario.

> Diana, the mother of a child who died, not only left the nursery untouched, but also kept it locked, to be opened only on the anniversary of the child's death. On this day, the surviving son and daughter were kept from school every year to pass a day in mourning. These two children, of disparate ages, had to share a room in order that the 'mourning room' should be kept immaculate. They resented their dead brother for preoccupying their mother to such an extent that their own needs were ignored.

In a way, clinging to grief makes it easier to bear. Like convalescence, the recovery is often the hardest part. The bereaved do not dare forget for a moment what has been lost; pain forgotten for that moment will come back to strike them down. The sea appears to be calm; then the unexpected wave hits them with full force, bowling them over and attempting to drown them again. In the book 'Continuing Bonds: New understandings of grief', several authors demonstrate that a healthy resolution of grief can enable one to maintain a continuing bond with the deceased; in fact this bond can enrich the lives of the bereaved. [1]

It is important that the path through mourning should be allowed to follow its course; that will not always occupy the same time span between couples, nor will it always follow the same path, but some day or another a new beginning has to be made. One of the reasons this is sometimes difficult to achieve is that recovery from grief and the renewal of everyday life are often accompanied by guilt. Mourning the death of his wife, C.S .Lewis says: *There's no denying that in some sense I 'feel better', and with that comes at once a sort of shame, and a feeling that one is under a sort of obligation to cherish and foment and prolong one's unhappiness.* [2] The bereaved mother cries: 'Am I forgetting my baby? What can I be thinking of?' Against this, some parents feel they want to forget entirely, and dispose of everything that will recall the lost child to mind. This is a pity, as good memories can be left behind to comfort the survivors. Such memories, however, can only materialize through the behaviour and reactions of other people connected to the parents during and following the death.

Whatever path through mourning the bereaved person takes, the path should be allowed to take its course. Philip Yancey tells the story of the grief pastor of a large church who also had two children of his own with life-threatening disorders. John said: *'We need to stay with the grief for a while, feel it, let it out. Maybe we can see things through tears that can't be seen dry-eyed.'* [3]

Practical moving on

There is a lot of practical tidying up to do following the death of a baby, with uncomfortable decisions to be made. Immediate decisions consist of funeral arrangements and choice of burial. The body must be consigned properly to an appropriate destination; for some this will mean burial, for others cremation. That is why the organ retention scandal was so painful for so many parents, even those who have no belief concerning the resurrection of the body intact after death; especially as, for some Muslims, the text from the Koran *'breaking the bone of the dead is akin to breaking the bone of the living'* could mean that there is a possibility the deceased could feel pain. [4]

It is difficult to understand the lack of imagination of those who delivered a body to the parents for burial, without even informing the parents that most, if not all, of the organs had been removed. Parents found they had wept at the graveside over the empty shell of a loved child. What could be done to put these memories right? Parents who discovered this had happened to their own babies were not left with happy memories.

Those close to the parents can help in the practical arrangements that have to be made. The parents may in their state of shock be quite incapable of caring for other children, cooking and housekeeping, and handling the details of the funeral such as where and who should arrange it, and who should be invited to attend. On the other hand, some parents may feel that active participation in practical tasks helps them to cope with their pain; if there is doubt about which of these is the case, the parents can be asked what they themselves prefer. Parents can remember that however helpless they feel they can speak of their fears, desires, and doubts. There is no shame in asking for help.

Children too need to be consulted when decisions are made concerning them. Sometimes, in an attempt to protect them from the pain of mourning, they are sent away from home, but this is not always a good idea. The children may then feel that they are in the way, unwanted, even rejected; when they witness their parents suffering, children often feel a sense of guilt at being the survivors. Again on the other hand, witnessing the anguish of their mother and father may be too daunting for little children; so when in doubt perhaps they could be asked what they themselves feel is best. Older children, too, have their rights as members of the family. It may help them to feel they are wanted, and offers of help should not be refused. But the life of a teenager does not wait for mourning; all support must continue for the adolescent child to study, take exams, engage in school activities. Co-operation, mutual support and sharing of tasks within a family can help to solidify a sense of unity.

Many funeral directors feel that it is best if the family can be involved in preparations for the funeral. They will inform the parents of the options open to them, and give them time to reach their decisions. In her book 'On the Death of a Child', Celia Hindmarch quotes one funeral director: *'I always try to take my instructions from the parents themselves, and encourage them to see and hold the child as often as they wish. If parents are reluctant to take the baby out of the coffin, I hold the baby myself first, to give them confidence and to show my respect.'* [5] 'Respect for the baby' – how good it is to hear that said – something to be remembered with warmth!

Other, less urgent decisions have to be made. What is to be done with little toys and clothes, gifts from friends, a room prepared as a nursery? Do these painful mementos get consigned to a trunk in the attic, given to a charity shop or to needy neighbours, or are they locked in a 'room of mourning', or even burnt? For many people, keeping the belongings collected for the coming baby is to tempt Providence – if there is a subsequent pregnancy, they prefer to start again. Other parents like to keep a Memory Box. The actual decision made does not really matter, provided that all concerned are in agreement, and that no one is left feeling resentful.

If there has been some question as to the cause of death, and in any case if the baby dies in hospital, the parents will wish to speak to a doctor. They may need reassurance –what has happened may occur again. There may be questions to be asked about future pregnancies. The question of post-mortem will have to be discussed, and in some cases permission asked for the retention of tissue for analysis. Or there may be questions as to methods of treatment – was the right thing done?

It is difficult for people following the shock of bereavement to take in what is being said to them, and it is often necessary for information to be repeated several times. Patience is needed, and understanding. Anger and suspicion, whether justified or not, need to be defused; they will not go away by themselves.

Sometimes the death of a baby is preceded by the difficult decision of whether a life should be prolonged. It is best if the parents together with all the medical team concerned in the child's care can share decision making, such as the discontinuing of life-support systems, but the parents need to be sure that the consultant is telling them the whole truth, that all possible has been done to save life. Such a decision cannot be made in a hurry; parents need time to absorb the shock of what is being told them. According to doctors A. R. Gatrad and A. Sheik, it may be easier for Muslim doctors to reach agreement with parents on the withdrawing of treatment, since Islamic teachings may be used in counselling: *We remind parents of God's Omnipotence and the transient nature of our earthly sojourn in contrast to the abiding reality of the hereafter.* [4]

Parents also need time to consult between themselves. It is sad when parents cannot agree, and when the convictions of one have to take precedence over the other. This can cause endless ill feeling, even lead to the permanent separation of the two. Unfortunately in matters of life and death there can be no compromise; but usually, if the consultant and the medical team are all in agreement and the parents have trust in everyone concerned, a decision can be reached without damage to relationships – sometimes they can even be strengthened, as the parents learn from their mutual dependence on each other. Above all, it is important that parents should not feel that the professionals have already taken a decision, and their own contribution to the discussion is illusory.

Doctors and nurses themselves frequently feel a sense of guilt at the death of a baby. They also ask: was the right thing done? Could more have been done? Or even, sometime, was too much done, and did the baby suffer? In any case, for doctors particularly death is often seen as a failure, and the death of a baby particularly so. Some are held back from frank discussion because they are afraid of the tears and the anger, not only those of the parents but also their own. This is a pity, as many parents appreciate empathy from doctors and nurses, and welcome the feeling that someone else cares. During my many years as a neonatal nurse, I found the greatest help at times of stress and disappointment came from my colleagues on the unit. At such times we can weep together, make each other cups of tea, comfort each other with shared experiences; these small things are for me much more valuable than sessions with a counsellor.

Physical moving on

Touching and feeling – how important this is in love! But sometimes when a baby dies the mother never gets a chance to see the child she has lost, let alone touch her and feel her. Alexa, whose baby was diagnosed as having a rare disorder incompatible with life, had to face a termination of pregnancy at twenty weeks; and saw her longed-for child delivered into a metal dish before being whisked away forever.

In order to make her real for them it is good if parents are able to see, touch and hold their dead child, but they should not be forced to do so. One doctor helped a mother to look at her stillborn baby by sitting on her bed and talking to her, with the child lying beside them wrapped in a green cloth: *'After a while, she was able to feel first the baby's foot through the cloth, and gradually the whole body; then the baby was uncovered.'* [6]

The parents of a baby who dies after birth have at least a chance to see and hold her, even to play their parental role; in neonatal units nowadays both parents are encouraged to help in the baby's care, if her condition allows it. They can learn nappy changing, gastric tube feeding, gentle stroking and massage. It must not be forgotten that babies respond to the sound of the human voice, particularly that of their mother, which they have learnt to recognise from the womb. Babies also have a sense of taste and smell; with the consent of the neonatal team, the mother can leave a breast pad nearby for the baby to smell, and can wipe her lips with a cotton bud soaked in her own milk for her to taste.

If the baby is so fragile that any touch would be too much for her to endure, there is one form of touch that can be beneficial. This is the 'containment' described in Chapter Five, the means by which a baby who seems stressed and anxious can be given comfort without stimulating or tiring her. The mother or father can thereby give their baby the comfort of their presence without asking her to give anything in return. In this way parents can regain a little control of their own baby. Since individual babies have ways of showing their feelings, the parents can learn to read her signals. If she seems fidgety and restless, and squirms when touched, they can take the positive action of taking away the touch and leaving her to rest, but if she lies quietly and relaxed she can be soothed by the warmth and gentleness of hands. Care of this practical sort given by parents at least leaves them with some personal knowledge of their baby, if she should eventually die.

Even in hospitals it is usually possible to offer the baby a dignified death. There are often rooms specially prepared for the parents and close family to use, where the parents may be with their dying child. They can hold her in their arms, freed from all the life-support equipment except what is necessary to keep her comfortable. The dying baby belongs to herself and to her parents, and they should be allowed to grieve alone unless they request otherwise; but parents may wish to have the company of trusted friends, relatives, or grandparents, who can help with their sympathy and support. Brothers and sisters of the baby can also be present at this time, even if they are quite small; very often they like to give their brother or sister a little gift or a drawing to take with them. Children are often pragmatic about death; to be together as a family will not seem strange to them at such a time, whereas to be left at home may leave them feeling rejected.

Some parents like to keep the baby with them after her death, and may like to bathe her and dress her in clothes they have brought themselves. Parents should be allowed to keep the baby with them as long as they wish (within reason), and should feel free to ask to see her again later if they feel the need. Many hospitals have a 'Moses basket' in which the baby, dressed in her own clothes and with little toys beside her, can lie beside the parents until they are ready to leave the ward. The Moses basket can also be reassuring to little children, since it gives them a feeling of familiarity, of 'domesticity'.

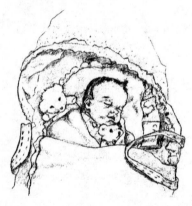

Some hospitals will make arrangements for parents to take the child to their own home to die if they so wish, if this will not cause added suffering to the baby – but there should be no constraint; there will be other parents who find this idea threatening and risky.

Even within families people do not always understand the importance of touch. Mark thought he was protecting his wife when he failed to suggest she should hold Lucy before she was taken from them. Nancy would have loved to have held her daughter one last time, but did not like to say so. By means of touching, and watching, and performing little services of care, the dying baby becomes real for the parents, and allows their memories of her to be of a presence, even if only for a short time.

While we are speaking of touch, something should be said on the subject of the resuming of sexual relations between the parents of the dead child. There is often an imbalance in the needs of couples at this time; the mother may prefer to be held and cuddled, but shudder away from sex, while the father has a need for sexual intimacy and fails to understand his partner's apparent coldness. Or indeed it can be the other way round; it is the mother who feels the need for sexual comfort, and the father who does not understand this and recoils. Patience with each other will only strengthen a relationship if there can be forbearance at this time.

Psychological moving on

'So many people came to the memorial service. It was all a little overwhelming. Family came from out of town as well as friends I did not expect to see. They were there to show their concern and love for us. It helps to be reminded of how much people love and care for us. And we still have each other,' wrote Christine O'Keeffe Lafser in her book 'An Empty Cradle, a Full Heart.' [7]

At last parents accept that their baby has left them; there is no longer a physical presence. But this does not mean the baby has to be forgotten. Sometimes it happens that immediately following a death the parents in their denial will hasten away from the hospital, putting away from them anything or anyone who will remind them of her. A photograph may be refused at first, but it is possible to take some photographs in any case, as they can always be set-aside for the parents to collect later if they change their minds; later they may be glad of such a keepsake. Hand prints and foot prints, the clothes and little toys the baby used, drawings made by siblings, records of any ceremony, can all be kept. Some parents like to save all such little mementos together in a Memory Box They can be looked at and touched until they are no longer needed and can be set aside. Once such a memorial has been put together with love and care, parents can then move on with their lives, and take up again with their old responsibilities and occupations.

Some people may find their ability to cope with grief is helped by 'rituals'. These may include such things as writing a journal, or an outpouring of anger in letters that are not sent to anyone but can be kept while needed and later destroyed, or putting aside time for daily periods of meditation with the use of candles or flowers.

Jenni Thomas, Founder and Director of the Child Bereavement Charity, has made a list of suggestions reflecting what parents feel to be most helpful in their interactions with professionals caring for children and babies who die. The professionals should remember that:

- parents need help to 'parent' before and after death

- parents need advice about pain control

- siblings need to be included in family discussions – they have something to offer

- nothing should be done without consulting parents (e.g. cutting a lock of hair for them to keep)

- honesty is a vital ingredient

- it should not be assumed that information given will be immediately understood

- full information should be given about the post-mortem

- parents should be allowed to have feelings

- patience is needed with parents who are in denial

- when organ donation is requested, the doctor should be specific to the parents about the pathologist's needs

- professionals should show parents they care – touching is the most basic form of communication and can pass language barriers

- in cases of sudden death, parents need time to absorb what is happening

- the culture and religious beliefs of the bereaved parents should be respected. People should be asked what they would like done.[8]

Nurses working on neonatal units have noticed that bereaved parents often make a pilgrimage to the unit on the anniversary of their baby's death, as though seeking comfort in the place where she had lived her life. People begin to cope with the aftermath of bereavement by helping others who are still travelling the same road. Sometimes the mothers and grandmothers of very tiny babies bring in little clothes; sometimes they bring knitted garments and blankets. Some mothers will even offer to work as volunteers in such a unit; some visit the mothers of other babies who are not going to live. In many districts, parents have set up local support groups, where people can meet and share their feelings and experiences. There are also national organisations that help bereaved parents and children come to terms with their grief, and a list of these will be found at the end of the book.

There are already books available for the guidance of bereaved parents and children, as well as books written by parents themselves expressing for the sake of others the pains and sorrows they endured, and how they managed to cope with their grief. As well as the references already quoted, a list of these will be found at the back of this book.

Spiritual moving on

I believe that when someone dies, we must pay attention to the departure (death) of the body and the existence (life) of the soul. There can often be satisfaction in the preparation of the bodies of people who have died. There is a respect, even love, in tending the tired flesh, restoring dignity and order to the face and body; it is the last service one can perform.

The beliefs and rites of the great religions of the world as they concern the death of babies can be tremendously supportive to believing parents, reassuring them that the essence of their baby still lives on, and will be reunited with them some day. In his encyclical letter, Pope Benedict writes: *'Baptism is not just an act of socialisation within the community, not simply a welcome into the church. Parents expect more for the one to be baptised: they expect that faith ... will give life to their child – eternal life.'* [9] It does sometimes happen, though, that a too strict attention to doctrine can sour this faith and the hope it brings.

As we have seen, there are still certain Christians who believe that babies cannot reach Paradise but are consigned to Limbo because they have not repented 'original sin.' Parents of babies who die are devastated by the thought of their babies disappearing into a dark place from which there is no return. What can one say to such parents? To make no effort to console them is to leave them unhappy; to express disagreement with this belief and to offer alternative hope is perhaps to break their faith completely. Hospital Chaplains have a difficult choice when asked to help people who hold such beliefs.

World religions have recognised that a name gives a person identity; it is very important for parents that their child should be named.

A couple belonging to the Anglican Church whose baby was dying in hospital asked for their baby to be baptised. They were not themselves regular churchgoers, but they contacted their local vicar and asked if he would officiate at the christening; he refused. His argument was that the promises made at baptism could not be met. By dying, this baby could not be part of the family of the church. The parents were devastated; they desperately wanted their son to be baptised. Eventually, without any difficulty, he was baptised by the hospital chaplain, but the bitterness felt at their vicar's coldness and rigid attention to doctrine remained with them, and left them forever mistrustful of the established church.

One father wrote a poem celebrating his daughter's short life, and asked to have it inscribed on the headstone for the grave. The vicar of the church refused to do this, since one line in the poem referred to her going 'into the dark', and according to the vicar this was not possible – she would be going 'into the light.' Again, the father was deeply hurt by this decision – to him, as to many of us, 'the dark' is not a place to be feared but a place warm and restful, a place for sleep.

There is a cemetery in North Wales where a local mason has prepared the headstones; they are covered with carvings of fairies, toys, television and Disney characters, little rhymes, and all the things beloved by the particular child. They may not be sophisticated or even in the best of taste, but they are strangely moving. Loving care has gone into the design of the stones, and the parents could have the feeling that the very best had been done to commemorate their children, dead too soon. The episode some years ago in a cemetery in Bristol, when more than 150 graves of babies and children were vandalised, and toys and flowers scattered and destroyed, has shown how much store parents set in the resting place of their children: 'What can we do? It will only happen again,' cried one distraught mother.

For parents who would like a permanent memorial, there is a practical guide 'Memorials by Artists for young people, children and babies' which explains how this can be done.[10]

It is particularly important for religious leaders of all faiths to be sensitive to the needs of bereaved parents, and to make sure that everything possible is done to ease their pain.

A young Jewish mother, Rebecca, was led to believe that no traditional mourning ceremony could be arranged for her son, since he died before thirty days had passed which would have led to his being legally regarded as a human being. She was bitterly angry to discover that her Rabbi had misled her when he told her no such ceremony could be performed. He failed to tell her that if only she had asked, a mourning ritual could have been arranged – and that was indeed what she most wished. Rebecca was left with a feeling of something unfinished, and is still overcome with rage when she remembers her frustration at this time.

Unfortunately, parents with such experiences will frequently not only be angry with the priest or rabbi, but will blame the God he purports to represent. It adds to the tragedy of the death of a baby when not only must the parents cope with their grief, but also find their belief shaken.

A happier story is that of the vicar who one summer's day was asked to conduct the funeral service of a newborn baby. Suddenly the young mother, who was feeling exhausted and faint, sank down on the grass by the open grave. The vicar sat down by her side, and suggested to the mourners that instead of supporting her to stand up again everyone should descend to her level. So they all sat down on the grass in the sunshine, and the rest of the service was conducted from there. The mother, who could even smile later when telling the tale, remembered with warmth this natural act of kindness.

Even if there is no formal funeral, many communities have little gardens of remembrance, which families can visit to leave flowers and to say a few prayers. For the religious, prayer is a powerful aid in overcoming grief, both their own prayers and those of friends, as is shown by Christine O'Keeffe Lafser in her book 'An Empty Cradle, A Full Heart': *People have been so kind. I can see the sadness in their eyes as they offer to help. There is nothing they can do, but they promise to keep us in their prayers. It helps to know that they care so much.'* [7]

In the first anguish of bereavement, however, it is hard to feel God's presence; indeed, he is conspicuous by his absence. 'Where were you, God, when my baby died? What was the point of it all?' The answer is silence. C. S. Lewis could write about this absence: *'Talk to me about the truth of religion and I'll listen gladly. Talk to me about the duty of religion and I'll listen submissively. But don't come talking to me about the consolations of religion or I shall suspect that you don't understand ... If a mother is mourning not for what she has lost but for what her dead child has lost, it is a comfort to believe that the child has not lost the end for which it was created ... it is a comfort to the God-aimed, eternal spirit within her. But not to her motherhood. The specifically maternal happiness must be written off. Never, in any place or time, will she have her son on her knees, or bath him, or tell him a story, or plan for his future, or see her grandchild.'* [2] **Never**, like **dead**, is another hard and diminishing word. There is no escaping 'never'.

Prayer

The Old Testament and the Torah show how to be in a rage with God. Prayer does not need to be polite; it can be an angry shouting and yelling at God, as did Job: *'I cry to you and you do not answer me; I stand, and you merely look at me. You have turned cruel to me; with the might of your hand you persecute me.'* [11] The Psalms are full of cries for help: *'How long, O Lord? Will you forget me forever? How long will you hide your face from me? How long must I bear pain in my soul, and have sorrow in my heart all day long'.* [12] For the Christian, St. Paul tells us in the Epistle to The Romans how even words are not needed to show our pain: *'the Spirit comes to the aid of our weakness. We do not even know how we ought to pray, but through our inarticulate groans the Spirit himself is pleading for us, and God who searches our inmost being knows what the spirit means.'* 13

Many of St. Paul's most exalted prayers were written in prison. Philip Yancey writes: *'A sceptic would see those prayers as reality-denial of the worst kind. A believer sees them as faith in a reality that transcends circumstances and disarms fear.'* 3 **Fear** (or perhaps dread is a better word) is also a part of mourning; the mourner wakes to grief and sleeps with grief – lives with foreboding – 'will it never end?'

But there are passages in Scripture of recovery from grief, also. Another Psalmist cries: *'You have turned my mourning into dancing; you have taken off my sackcloth and clothed me with joy.'* 14 And finally, there is the famous promise from the Revelation of St. John, used for comfort at funeral services: *'He will wipe every tear from their eyes. Death will be no more; mourning and crying and pain will be no more.'* 15

Islam teaches that pain can be accepted, since everything belongs to Allah, and will return to Allah: *'...What Allah takes belongs to Him, what He gives belongs to Him, and He has an appointed time for everyone...'* 16The Koran comforts the believer: *'Have We not lifted up your heart and relieved you of the burden which weighed down your back? ... Every hardship is followed by ease.'* 17

Prayer is common to all the religions, and often people of little or no faith will ask for prayers or themselves pray in desperation. Christine O'Keeffe Lafser tells of one mother's use of prayer following her baby's death: *'Some people say it is a shame. Others even imply that it would have been better if the baby had never been created. But the short time I had with my child is precious to me. It is painful now, but I still wouldn't wish it away... I am proud that we co-operated with God in the creation of a new soul for all eternity. Although not with me, my baby lives.'* 7

Memories are all that is left for the parents of a baby who dies; all the warmth generated by the sensitive and caring support of doctors, nurses, friends and family during the dying and death of the baby will be as nothing if later they feel lost and abandoned. The funeral is over, but that does not mean that no ceremony can ever take place again. The parents of children who die feel themselves to be special – their grief is so peculiarly different from grief felt for people who have lived a complete life. Sadly, frequently parents feel this grief is not recognised, and this gives them a sense of isolation. Now, many hospitals organise annual or bi-annual ecumenical memorial services for bereaved parents, and these are well attended by people of all faiths and none. They gather together afterwards for a cup of tea, and in sharing their stories, and meeting members of the staff who cared for their baby, they can comfort themselves that the 'caring' has not ceased.

Such a ceremony is 'A Celebration of Life,' a leaflet written by Caroline Jay that describes the organisation of a service of remembrance for babies and children.[18] Following the death of her daughter Laura, she was too shocked to arrange the funeral, and was disappointed in the meaningless and impersonal service that she was offered. Four years later, her own church came to her rescue and arranged a little service for Laura.

She says: *When your world has just fallen apart, it is not easy to make decisions. Those who had miscarriages may have been unsure as to what to do. Those bereaved longer ago would not even have been given any decisions to make. Their babies would have been whisked away and incinerated before there was any chance to say goodbye. For the sake of all these people, I decided to ask for the church's help. I decided to try and arrange a service for all babies and children loved and lost at any stage in pregnancy and at any age in life.'* [18] So that is precisely what she did.

Many parents who do not hold a funeral and have no grave or memorial to visit lack a focus for their grief (this often happens following miscarriage). As time passes, they feel a sense of 'unfinished business', and that there has been no proper conclusion to their mourning. This feeling can persist over the years. Many times, women will tell of their own long-drawn-out pain – sometimes going back forty years or more. Sometimes for people who feel this emptiness, services and ceremonies such as the one described above can be arranged many years later and these belated ceremonies can be a relief to parents, who feel they can now 'lay their grief to rest'.

Now that the intense grieving is past, and the parents have accepted that their baby has died, they can also accept that the baby was a real person, flesh, blood and soul, did live, was loved, was lost, but somewhere is still present. They can remember without guilt or fear, in the knowledge that her short life was recognised, that it was not all for nothing. Sadly, too many parents are frustrated by the failure of family, friends and professionals to see the lost baby as a person who has existed, even if the death took place before the baby could be born.

Karen Holford in her book 'The Loneliest Grief' described the experiences of one old lady of 80, who had had a miscarriage at the age of 20. *'At the time everyone said the usual things to her: "Pull yourself together and get on with your life, dear"; "Oh, you'll soon have another one" and so on. So she never spoke about her experiences to anyone for sixty years.'* But in sixty years she had never forgotten, *"'for all this time I have been crying inside, and sometimes outside too, when no one was around. Now you have let me talk about it, and listened, and understood. Now I'm beginning to feel some healing inside".'* [19]

Perhaps the greatest release from the pain of grief is the ending of the long silence. Peggy Orenstein remarks '*...even in this era of compulsive confession, women don't speak publicly of their loss. It is only if your pregnancy is among the unlucky ones that fail that you begin to hear stories, spoken in confidence, almost whispered. Your aunt, your grandmother. Your friends. Your colleagues. Women you have known for* *years — sometimes your whole life — who have had this happen, sometimes over and over and over again. They tell only if you become one of them.'* [20] Many people, women as well as men, find it impossible to express their sense of desolation to anyone else, perhaps because of their own frozen state, more often because of difficulty in finding someone who will truly listen. Those closest, bereaved themselves, are not always the best comforters. There is a great need for an unburdening of the spirit, which can find release in strange ways.

Mary's first baby was born with a heart malformation that required expensive surgery. It was an operation that had been done successfully before, but sadly Mark died shortly afterwards. There was no blame; Mary was satisfied with the care Mark had received, but she could not get over the loss of her baby; her grief went on and on. As time passed, she found it difficult to talk about Mark any more, even to her husband, so she kept silent about the ache in her heart, while the people around her took up their lives again.

One day Mary was walking alone in a country lane, when she saw coming towards her an elderly man with a dog. Suddenly, as he drew abreast, Mary found herself telling him the whole story of Mark's illness and death – the words flowed out of her. The old man bent his head towards her, and listened until she finally ran out of words and came to an end. Then, she thanked him, and they both continued on their way, each going in the opposite direction to the other. She never saw him again.

Afterwards, thinking about the episode, Mary felt guilty at what she perceived as an infliction of her own personal pain onto a complete stranger. She was afraid that perhaps the man might have been hurt and upset by having to listen to such a tragic story. But he was old and must have suffered bereavement himself, maybe many times. It is more likely that he felt honoured by her trust, and gratified that he could be so useful to someone in pain. Or, perhaps, he was her angel for that day.

Mary's grief was profound; somehow, being able to pour out her heart in spoken words had eased her, and she felt more able to return to her family and their everyday life together. She told no one of the encounter, but she never forgot it and years later felt able to tell her story to another stranger.

After the initial shock and despair begin to dissipate, bereaved parents feel the need to communicate with the outside world. This is when the immediate circle of the family, close friends, and professionals who have cared for the baby and the parents, show their true worth. Moving on does not mean oblivion. Now is the time for the sympathetic listener. Expert professional help from bereavement counsellors, religious leaders, psychiatrists and social workers can be invaluable, but no great skill is needed to listen and to empathise. People frequently feel they are clumsy and embarrassed in the face of mourning, but loving attention to the outpourings of bewilderment, rage and sorrow is all that is needed to help ease the pain of an overburdened heart. This loving attention will be remembered. As one bereaved mother said, 'Some people said the wrong thing, some people didn't know what to say, but we could forgive their clumsiness because we could see they cared about what happened to us, and they cared about our son, and that is what mattered.'

A man once stood in prayer
his heart breaking from the pain
and injustice in the world.
'Dear God', he cried out,
'look at all the suffering,
the anguish and distress in the world.
Why don't you send help?'
God responded, 'I did send help.
I sent you.'

From: Zulu Mission News

References:

1. Klass D., Silverman P.R., Nickman S.L., (1996), *Continuing Bonds: New understandings of grief.* Taylor and Francis, London.

2. Lewis, C.S. (1961) *A Grief Observed.* Faber & Faber Limited, London.

3. Yancey, P. (2006) *Prayer: does it make any difference?* Hodder & Stoughton, London

4. Gatrad, A.R & Sheikh, A. (2001): *Medical Ethics and Islam: principles and practice.* In: Archives of Disease in Childhood: **84**:72-75

5. Hindmarch, C. (1993) *On the Death of a Child.* Radcliffe Medical Press, Oxford.

6. Jolly, H. (1975) *Book of Child Care.* George Allen & Unwin, London.

7. O'Keeffe Lafser, C. (1998) *An Empty Cradle, A Full Heart.* Loyola Press, Chicago.

8. Thomas, J. *Baby and Child Death: Managing the Issues.* The Child Bereavement Charity Conference, The Queen Elizabeth Hall, London. 15th May, 2001.

9. *Encyclical letter of Pope Benedict (November 2007),* The Vatican, Rome.

10. Frazer, H. & Meynell, H. (eds.) (2005) *Memorials by Artists.* Memorials by Artists Ltd., Snape, Suffolk.

11. *The Revised English Bible,* The book of Job 30:20-21. Oxford University Press.

12. Ibid. Psalm 13:1-2

13.   Ibid. St. Paul's Epistle to the Romans 8:26-27

14.   Ibid. Psalm 30:1

15.   Ibid. Revelation of St. John 21:21-24

16.   Eaton, G. (1994) *Islam and the Destiny of Man.* The Islamic Texts Society, Cambridge

17.   Comfort, 94:1 *The Koran,* (1974) Translated by Dawood, N.J. Revised Edition, Penguin Classics, Harmondsworth, Middlesex

18.   Jay, C. *A Celebration of Life.* (Obtainable from The Child Bereavement Charity, see 'Useful addresses.)

19.   Holford, K. (1994) *The Loneliest Grief.* Autumn House Publications, Grantham.

20.   Orenstein, P. (2002) *Mourning My Miscarriage.* The New York Times Magazine, April 21.

APPENDIX 1

From Sparshott, M. (1997) Pain, Distress and the
Newborn Baby, Blackwell Science, Oxford.

Model of nursing based on human needs for a newborn baby within the hospital environment
To cherish: to protect and treat with affection: to nurture, nurse. (*Chambers Twentieth Century Dictionary*)

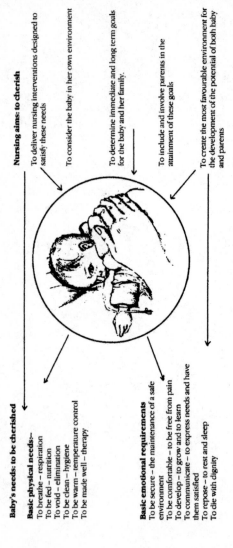

Nursing aims: to cherish

To deliver nursing interventions designed to satisfy these needs

To consider the baby in her own environment

To determine immediate and long term goals for the baby and her family.

To include and involve parents in the attainment of these goals

To create the most favourable environment for the development of the potential of both baby and parents

Baby's needs: to be cherished

Basic physical needs:--
To breathe – respiration
To be fed – nutrition
To void – elimination
To be clean – hygiene
To be warm – temperature control
To be made well – therapy

Basic emotional requirements
To be secure – the maintenance of a safe environment
To be comfortable – to be free from pain
To develop – to grow and to learn
To communicate – to express needs and have them satisfied
To repose – to rest and sleep
To die with dignity

Goal: To establish the most propitious environment for physical growth, learning and the development of identity.

182

APPENDIX 2

CATEGORIES OF ENVIRONMENTAL DISTURBANCE AND THEIR TREATMENT -1:

DISTURBANCE

From Sparshott, M. (1994) Nursing Care of a baby in pain and discomfort. In: Neonatal Nursing (eds D. Crawford & M. Morris). Chapman and Hall, London.

PAIN	DISCOMFORT	DISTURBANCE
- Intubation	- Monitoring	- Light
- Chest drain insertion and removal	- Physical examination	- Noise
	- Extubation	- Cold
-Venepuncture	- Range finding, due to insecutity	- Heat
- Heel-prick		- Nappy change
- Suctioning		- Position change
- I.M. injection	- Chest physiotherapy	- Nakedness
- Wound cleansing	- Electrode removal	- Weighing
- CPAP	- Rectal temperature	- Overhandling
- Lumbar puncture	- Passage of NG or OG-tube	- Feeding by NG or OG-tube
- Arterial or suprapubic stab	- I.V. medication	-Bottle feeding when too weak
- Surgery	- Splinting	- Isolation
- Illness, e.g. meningitis, necrotizing entercolitis	- Physical restraint	- Separation
	- Phototherapy	-Lack of stimulation, if well
	- Urine bag removal	- Noxious taste/odour
	- Adhesive tape removal	
	- Hunger	

CATEGORIES OF ENVIRONMENTAL DISTURBANCE AND THEIR TREATMENT -2:

TREATMENT

THERAPY	CONSOLATION	CHERISHMENT
- **Prevent pain by:** • Technique • Preparation before hand • Abstention • Grouping care - **Treat pain by** • Analgesia • Local anaesthetic • Anaesthetic cream - **Treat intractable pain by:** • Relief of symptoms • Containment • Narcotic analgesia	- Music and sound - Provision of boundaries - Containment - Stroking and massage - Swaddling - Rocking - Non-nutritive sucking - Breastfeeding - Encouragement of self consolation (hand-to-mouth movement) - Encasement - Correct positioning	- Day and Night lighting - Noise reduction - Minimal handling or stimulation - Clothing and coverings - Parental presence - Soft toys - Musical toys and cassettes/CDs - Pictures - Mirrors - Mobiles - Baby carriers - Baby chairs - Skin-to-skin contact - Pleasant taste/odour

APPENDIX 3

SIGNS OF STRESS AND WELL-BEING

From Sparshott, M. (1997) Pain, Distress and the Newborn Baby, Blackwell Science, Oxford.

Signs of stress

- Crying
- 'Grimacing', making faces
- Eyes squeezed tightly closed
- Excessive coughing, sneezing, yawning
- Hiccoughing, gagging, vomiting
- Fingers splayed – hands appear 'star shaped'
- Either – extreme limpness, flaccidity
- or – frantic activity, violent movements of limbs
- Tremors, 'startles', twitches
- Very uneven breathing, pauses in respiration
- Colour changes – becomes pale, mottled, grey or blue

Note: babies are lively and changeable creatures, and may show many of these as signs of energy and activity – for instance, all babies are sick from time to time, and finger splay may simply be the exercise of stretching – but it is when these signs are repeated frequently, or are seen together, that the baby may be showing he is stressed. The cause for the stress must then be found.

Ways to soothe and comfort your baby

- Talk to him in a gentle voice – sing to him!
- Stroke his body and/or limbs
- Gently stroke his forehead
- 'Contain' his head and body in your hands*
- Hold his hand – let him grasp your fingers
- After he has been disturbed, place him in his preferred position
- Tuck or cuddle him into his blanket
- Cuddle him, holding him close to you with his head supported (not with his head on his chest, which would impede his breathing!)
- Hold him to nestle against your shoulder
- Rock him in your arms
- Give him something to suck (if he can do so)
- Bring him a cassette of your own voice to comfort him when you are unable to be there

* (Containment)   If your baby seems stressed and anxious, but is very small and fragile, you can give him comfort without stimulating him. Without moving your baby, gently cup your hand over the top and back of his head. Then place your other hand lightly over his trunk, so that you are 'holding' him without stimulating him. By doing this, you are giving your baby the comfort of your presence without asking him to give anything in return.

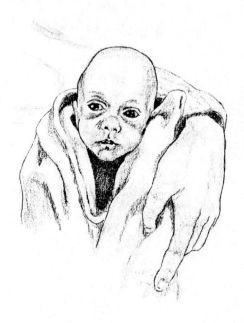

Signs of a state of well-being.

- A relaxed and comfortable position
- Peaceful sleep – no rapid eye movement
- Eyes open and intent, alert appearance
- Head and eyes turned towards sound of voice
- Movements smooth and coordinated, not jerky
- Hand will clasp a finger
- Hands relaxed with fingers folded
- 'Preening' movement of body when stroked
- Movement of hand to mouth
- Sucking or rooting movement
- A good, even colour of skin
- Breathing is even, not irregular or laboured

Ways to stimulate your baby (when she is ready)

- Talk to her, while looking into her face from about 10 inches away
- Stroke her**
- Sing to her
- Bring small soft toys which she can grasp
- Bring little books or pictures with brightly coloured designs (or black and white) for her cot
- Bring a lullaby music box to play after feeds, before she goes to sleep
- Bring cassettes of restful, rhythmical music
- Play with her at bath times, stretching and massaging her limbs***
- More mature babies may enjoy looking at mobiles

** 'Stroking' is done by sliding the fingers lightly along the surface of the skin

*** 'Massaging' is done by using the fingers to move the muscles beneath the skin. To begin with, use the lightest 'feather' touch until you see how the baby likes it. Massage from top to toe, and don't forget to include both arms and both legs, so that your baby doesn't feel unbalanced! If you have long fingernails and don't want to cut them, make sure you use only the balls of your fingers and the palms of your hands.

A useful book on baby massage: Walker, P. (1995) *Baby Massage*. Judy Piatkus (Publishers) Ltd., London.

APPENDIX 4

LAYING THE FOUNDATIONS: CARING FOR BEREAVED FAMILIES IN HOSPITAL

From CDCA (Constructive Dialogue of Clinical Accountability) CDCA Charity No. 1085419. 54, Alma Vale Road, Cliffton, Bristol B58 2HS.

C are and compassion are key elements. Do you have these qualities?

O ffer yourself as a fellow human-being, listening carefully and actively. Remember – your body language will convey what you are thinking.

M essage of grief: recognition that the pain of grief cannot be taken away. There are no instant solutions and therefore there are no hard and fast rules for how to respond.

P rocedures: each Unit should have practical guidelines to help you. When possible, read these before a death occurs to help you feel more confident.

A ccept the parents' reactions. Can you deal with anger or silence?

S eek help, if possible, if you feel overwhelmed or out of your depth.

S upervision/support should be available to you. Ensure that you have sufficient time to debrief and learn from each situation.

I nformation is important to parents. Clear, written guidelines to help parents after death and information and leaflets on relevant voluntary organisations should be available.

O ffer choices to parents to help them make informed decisions.

N otify community health care professionals so that they may continue the care you have started.

FURTHER READING

For those who mourn

All in the End is Harvest. (1994) Edited Whitaker, A. Dartman, Longman & Todd, London. (An anthology)

Lewis, C.S. (1961) *A Grief Observed.* Faber and Faber Ltd., London. (A personal testimony written following the death of his wife.)

Saunders, C. (1983) *Beyond All Pain.* SPCK, London. (An anthology)

Words of Comfort (2000, 2nd edition) compiled by Herbert, C. National Society/Church House Publishing, London. (An anthology)

For parents

Bradford, N. (1998) *The Miraculous World of Your Unborn Baby.* Bramley Books, Quadrillion Publishing Ltd., Godalming, Surrey.

Dillon, J. (1990) *A Path to Hope: for parents of aborted children and those who minister to them.* Resurrection Press, New York

Goodall, J. (1995) *Children and Grieving.* Scripture Union, London.

Holford, K. (1994) *The Loneliest Grief.* Autumn House Publications, Grantham.

Jay, C. (1995) *A Celebration of Life*, a leaflet available from the Child Bereavement Charity (See 'Useful Addresses')

Kohner, N. & Henley, A. (1995 revised edition) *When a Baby Dies.* HarperCollins, London.

Kohner, N. & Thomas, J. (1995) *Grieving after the death of your baby.* The Child Bereavement Charity (See 'Useful Addresses)

Lister, M. & Lovell, S. (1991) *Healing Together: For Couples Grieving the Death of Their Baby*. Centering Corporation, Omaha, NE.

O'Keeffe Lafser, C. (1998) *An Empty Cradle, a Full Heart*. Loyola Press, Chicago.

Storkey, E. (1989) *Finding a Path Through the Pain*. LION publishing plc, Oxford.

Warden, A. (1999) *Benedict: a Child of Mine*. The Child Bereavement Charity, High Wycombe, Bucks. (A mother's personal experience expressed in poetry) (See 'Useful Addresses)

For children

Goble, P. (1993) *Beyond the Ridge*. Aladdin Books, Macmillan Publishing Company, New York.

Stickney, D. (1984) *Waterbugs and Dragonflies*. The Pilgrim Press, Mowbray, London.

Varley, S. (1985) *Badger's Parting Gifts*. Andersen Press, London.

For professional carers

Bagness, C. (1998) *Genetics, the Fetus and our Future*. Hochland & Hochland Ltd., Hale, Cheshire.

Brewin, T. with Sparshott, M. (1996) *Relating to the Relatives*. Radcliffe Medical Press, Oxford.

Continuing Bonds: New Understandings of Grief (1996): (Eds. Klass D., Silverman P.R., & Nickman S.L.), Taylor & Francis, London.

Leon, I.G. (1990) *When a Baby Dies*. Yale University Press, New Haven and London. (psychotherapy for pregnancy and newborn loss)

McHaffie, H. (2001) *Crucial Decisions at the Beginning of Life*. Radcliffe Medical Press, Oxford.

Neuberger, J. (1994) *Caring for Dying People of Different Faiths* (2nd edition). Mosby, Times Mirror International Publishers Ltd., London.

Sparshott, M.M. (1997) *Pain, Distress and the Newborn Baby*. Blackwell Science, Oxford.

Thomas, J. (1993) *Supporting Parents when their Baby Dies.* A guide for staff – antenatal, labour ward, postnatal gynaecological and neonatal teams.

Religion

Atkinson, D. (1985) *Life and Death: Moral Choices and the Beginning and End of a Life.* (Part of the series: *Studies in Christianity and Science.*) Oxford University Press, Oxford.

Fisher, M..P (1997) *Living Religions.* I.B.Taurus and Co. Ltd., London.

A New Dictionary of Christian Theology (1983) (eds. Richardson, A. and Bowden, J.) SCM Press Ltd., London.

Parrinder, G. (1964) *The World's Living Religions.* Pan Books Ltd., London.

Schott, J. and Henley, A. (1996) *Culture, Religion and Childbearing in a Multiracial Society.* Butterworth-Heinemann, Oxford.

VIDEOS

When our Baby Died. – A video for parents, their families and those who care for them.

Death at Birth – miscarriage, stillbirth, neonatal death and termination for abnormality. A two part training video and accompanying booklet for professionals.

These videos and accompanying booklet may be obtained from the Child Bereavement Charity. (See 'Useful Addresses')

USEFUL ADDRESSES

The British Association for Counselling and Psychotherapy.

15 St John's Road,
Lutterworth LE17 4HB
Tel: 01455 883 300
www.bacp.co.uk

Child Bereavement Charity.

Aston House, High Street, West Wycombe, High Wycombe, Bucks. HP14 3AG

Tel: 01494 446 648
Fax. 01494440057
www.childbereavement.org.uk

Offers support and information for bereaved families and the professionals who support them, and training courses, workshops and seminars for families and professionals.

CBC Shop with a large selection of resources for families and professionals, either online or from above address.

Child Death Helpline

Admin (London): 020 7813 8551
Admin: (Liverpool) 0151 252 5391
Helpline: 0800 282 986

A confidential helpline run from the Great Ormond Street Hospital for Children in London and from the Alder Hey Centre,

Liverpool. Support for anyone affected by the death of a child, at any age, from any cause.

The Compassionate Friends

53 North Street, Bristol BS3 1EN

Tel: 08451 203 785   Fax: 08451 203 786

From Overseas:

Tel: +44 117 966 5202   Fax:: +44 117 914 4368

A nationwide self-help organisation for bereaved parents; resource library and advice leaflets.

The Compassionate Friends Sibling Support

Helpline: 0845 123 2304

info@cfsiblingssupport.org.uk

Cruse Bereavement Care

PO Box 800, Richmond, Surrey TW9 1RG
Tel: 020 8939 9530
Helpline: 0844 477 9400

Support and counselling for all bereaved people.

Foundation for the Study of Infant Deaths

11 Belgrave Road, London SW1V 1RB
Tel: General: 0207 802 3200
Helpline 080 8802 6868 (freephone)

Support and information for families bereaved through sudden infant death (cot death).

Jeremiah's Journey.

Jeremiah's Journey is a Plymouth based grief support programme for children, adolescents and their parents who have lost or are anticipating losing someone precious to them through death.

www. Jeremiah's Journey.org.uk
info@jeremiahsjourney.org.uk

Jewish Bereavement Counselling Service

Bet Meir,

Tel. 02084579710
Fax. 02084579707
jbcs@jvisit.org.uk

Support for Jewish parents who have experienced a stillbirth or a neonatal death.

Memorials by Artists Ltd.,

Snape Priory, Snape, Suffolk IP17 1SA
Memorials by artists for young people, children and babies.

The Miscarriage Association

C/o Clayton Hospital, Northgate, Wakefield, West Yorkshire WF1 3JS.

Tel: Admin 01924 200 795   Helpline: 01924 200 799

Support and information for those affected by pregnancy loss (including healthcare professionals.)

Royal College of Nursing Counselling and Advisory Service

Counselling Service: **Tel: 0845 769 7064**

Stillbirth and Neonatal Death Society (SANDS)

28 Portland Place, London W1B 1LY.

Tel: Admin: 020 7436 7940
Helpline: 020 7436 5881   **www.uk-sands.org**

Support and information for parents whose babies die before, during or after birth. Information, support and training for professionals.

Rainbow Trust's Children's Charity:

6 Cleeve Court, Cleeve Road, Leatherhead, Surrey, KT227UD.

Tel: 01372 363 438

Fax: 01372 363 101

enquiries@rainbowtrust.org.uk

www.rainbowtrust.org.uk

Rainbow Trust's Children's Charity provides practical and emotional support to families who have a child with a life-threatening or terminal illness. It offers support to families from diagnosis to long-term post-bereavement.

Winston's Wish

Helpline: 08452030405
info@winsotneswish.org.uk

Help for grieving children

BIBLIOGRAPHY

Chapter 1. What is a Baby?

Ali YA. (1938) *The Meaning of the Glorious Quran* 33:5. Cairo: Dar-al-kitab. (Translation modified)

Bradford, N. (1998) *The Miraculous World of Your Unborn Baby.* Bramley Books. Quadrillion Publishing Ltd., Godalming, Surrey.

Bryant, J. & Searle, J. (2004) Life in Our Hands. Inter-Varsity Press, Leicester.

Holford, K. (1994) *The Loneliest Grief.* Autumn House Publications, Grantham.

Jones, H.W, Veeck, L. (2002) What is an embryo? In: *Fertility and Sterility,* **vol.77**, no.4. p. 658-659

Sparshott, M. (1997) *Pain, Distress and the Newborn Baby.* Blackwell Science, Oxford.

Wolke, D. (1987) Environmental and developmental neonatology. *Journal of Reproductive and Infant Psychiatry,* **5**, 17-42.

Chapter 2.   The Mourning Process

Brewin, T. with Sparshott, M.M. (1996) *Relating to the Relatives.* Radcliffe Medical Press, Oxford.

Hindmarch, C. *On the Death of a Child.* Radcliffe Medical Press, Oxford.

Klaus, M.H. & Kennell, J.H. (1976) *Maternal-Infant Bonding.* C.V.Mosby, St. Louis.

Lindemann, E. (1944) Symptomatology and management of acute grief. *American Journal of Psychiatry,* **101**, 141-8.

Sparshott, M.M. (1997) *Pain, Distress and the Newborn Baby.* Blackwell Science, Oxford.

Chapter 3. Death before Birth

Brewin, T. with Sparshott, M.M. (1996) The angry relative. In: *Relating to the Relatives*. Radcliffe Medical Press.

Dillon, J.J. (1990) *A Path to Hope*. Resurrection Press, Mineola, New York.

Leon, I.G. (1990) *When a Baby Dies*. Yale University Press, New Haven and London.

Sparshott, M.M. (1990) The human touch. *Paediatric Nursing*, **2**(5), 8 – 10.

Sparshott, M.M. (1997) *Pain, Distress and the Newborn Baby*. Blackwell Science, Oxford.

Chapter 4.   Death at Birth

Brewin, T. with Sparshott, M.M. (1996) The angry relative. In: *Relating to the Relatives,* Radcliffe Medical Press.

Kohner, N. & Henley, A. (1995) *When a Baby Dies.* Routledge, London. (2nd Edition)

Leon, I.G. (1990) *When a Baby Dies.* Yale University Press, New Haven and London.

O'Keeffe Lafser, C. (1998) *An Empty Cradle, A Full Heart.* Loyola Press, Chicago.

Chapter 5. Death After Birth

Als, H. (1986) A synactive model of neonatal behavioural organization. *Physical and Occupational Therapy in Pediatrics*, **6**, 3-53.

Kohner, N & Henley, A. *When a Baby Dies:* The experiences of late miscarriage and neonatal death. Pandora Press, HarperCollins Publishers, London.

Sparshott, M.M. (1997) P*ain, Distress and the Newborn Baby.* Blackwell Science, Oxford.

Chapter 6.   The Family

Avery, G. (2000)   Intimations of Mortality: The Puritan and Evangelical Message to Children. In: *Representations of Childhood Death.* (Eds. Avery, G. & Reynolds, K.),

Brewin, T. with Sparshott, M. (1996) *Relating to the Relatives.* Radcliffe Medical Press, Oxford.

Goodall, J. (1995) *Children and Grieving.* Scripture Union, London.

Hindmarch, C. (1993) *On the Death of a Child.* Radcliffe Medical Press, Oxford.

Morris, M. (1994) Neonatal care today. *In: Neonatal Nursing* (eds D. Crawford & M. Morris). Chapman & Hall, London.

Paediatric Intensive Care Society (2002) *Standards for Bereavement Care 2002.* Obtainable from: Dr. C.G.Stack, Honorary Secretary, PICU, Sheffield Children's Hospital, Western Bank, Sheffield S10 2TH.

Chapter 7   What went wrong?

Baby and Child Death – Managing the Issues. The Child Bereavement Charity Conference, May 2001.

Sudden Death – Shattered Lives. The Child Bereavement Charity Conference, June 2002.

Begley, C. (2003: 'I cried ... I had to ...' Student midwives' experiences of stillbirth, miscarriage and neonatal death. *Evidence Based Midwifery,* Vol.1, pp20-26

Brewin, T. with Sparshott, M. (1996) *Relating to the Relatives: breaking bad news, communication and support.* Radcliffe Medical Press, Oxford.

Yancey, P. (1998) *Where is God When it Hurts?* Marshall Pickering, HarperCollins *Religious,* London.

Chapter 8. The Destination of the Body.

Schott, J. and Henley, A. (1996): *Culture, Religion and Childbearing in a Multiracial Society*, Butterworth-Heinemann, Oxford.

Chapter 9   The Existence of the Soul

Atkinson, D. (1985) *Life and Death: Moral Choices and the Beginning and End of a Life.* (Part of the series: *Studies in Christianity and Science.*) Oxford University Press, Oxford.

Eaton, Gai (1994): *Islam and the Destiny of Man.* The Islamic Text Society, Cambridge.

Kolatch, Alfred J. (1998): *The Jewish Book of WHY.* Jonathan David Publishers Inc., New York.

Knott, Fr. Peter. S.J. (1989) *Safe in God's Hands: Healing the hurt of losing your baby.* Incorporated Catholic Truth Society, London.

Koran, The (1974): Translated by Dawood, N.J. Revised edition, Penguin Classics, Harmondsworth, Middlesex.

Krishnamurti, Jiddu (1973) *The Awakening of Intelligence.* Harper & Row, New York.

A New Dictionary of Christian Theology (1983): (eds. Richardson, A. & Bowden, J.) SCM Press Ltd., London.

Neuberger, J. (1994) *Caring for Dying People of Different Faiths* (2nd ed.). Mosby, Times Mirror International Publishers Ltd., London.

Parrinder, G. (1964): *The World's Living Religions,* Pan Books Ltd., London.

Sanatana-Dharma: an elementary text-book of Hindu religion and ethics (1980): The Theosophical Publishing House, Madras, India.

Schott, J. and Henley, A. (1996): *Culture, Religion and Childbearing in a Multiracial Society*, Butterworth-Heinemann, Oxford.

Sookhedeo, P. (2001) *The Christian's Pocket Guide to Islam.* Christian Focus Publications, Geanies House, Fearn, Scotland

and Isaac Publishing, The Old Rectory, River Street, Pewsey, Wilts.

Sparshott, M. (2004): *The spirituality of babies*: respecting the religious beliefs of bereaved parents. Journal of Neonatal Nursing, **10,** Issue 5. p. 152-155

Walpola Sri Rahula (1974): *What the Buddha Taught* (revised edition), Grove Press, New York.

Chapter 10   Holy Innocents

Atkinson, D. (1985) *Life and Death: Moral Choices and the Beginning and End of a Life.* (Part of the series: *Studies in Christianity and Science.*) Oxford University Press, Oxford.

Eaton, Gai (1994): *Islam and the Destiny of Man.* The Islamic Text Society, Cambridge.

Festal Menaion, The (1969) Translated from the Greek by Mother Mary and Archimendrite Kallistos Ware. Faber and Faber, London.

Gatrad, A.R & Sheikh, A. (2001): *Medical Ethics and Islam: principles and practice.* In: Archives of Disease in Childhood: **84**:72-75

Khan, Hazrat Inayat (2000): *The Wisdom of Sufism – Sacred Readings from the Gathas.* Element Books Ltd, Shaftsbury, Dorset.

Kolatch, Alfred J. (1998): *The Jewish Book of WHY.* Jonathan David Publishers Inc., New York.

Konick, L. (2006): *Welcome Your Baby:* (Faith traditions), www.belief.net. Beliefnet, Inc.

Koran, The (1974): Translated by Dawood, N.J. Revised edition, Penguin Classics, Harmondsworth, Middlesex.

Nash, R.E. (1999) *When a Baby Dies.* Zondervan Publishing House, Grand Rapids, Michigan.

A New Dictionary of Christian Theology (1983): (eds. Richardson, A. & Bowden, J.) SCM Press Ltd., London.

Parrinder, G. (1964): *The World's Living Religions,* Pan Books Ltd., London.

Saddhatissa, H. (1976): *The Life of Buddha.* Unwin Paperbacks, George Allen & Unwin Ltd, London.

Sanatana-Dharma: an elementary text-book of Hindu religion and ethics (1980): The Theosophical Publishing House, Madras, India.

Schott, J. and Henley, A. (1996): *Culture, Religion and Childbearing in a Multiracial Society*, Butterworth-Heinemann, Oxford.

Sparshott, M. (2004): *The spirituality of babies*: respecting the religious beliefs of bereaved parents. Journal of Neonatal Nursing, **10,** Issue 5. p. 152-155

Tarazi, N. (1995): *The child in Islam.* Indiana: ATP. Pp42-46

Walpola Sri Rahula (1974): *What the Buddha Taught* (revised edition), Grove Press, New York.

Ware, T. (1963): *The Orthodox Church.* Penguin Books, Harmondsworth, Middlesex.

Chapter 11.   Moving On.

Al-Asqalani AIH. (1996) *Bulugh al-Maram.* Dar-us-Salam Publications, Riyadh. pp199-200

Brewin, T., with Sparshott, M.M. (1996) *Relating to the Relatives.* Radcliffe Medical Press, Oxford.

Childs-Gowell, E. (1992) *Good Grief Rituals.* Station Hill Press, Barrytown, New York. (In the U.K.: Smallwood Publishing Ltd., Dover, Kent.)

Continuing Bonds: New Understanding of Grief (1996): (Eds. Klass D., Silverman P.R., & Nickman S.L.), Taylor & Francis, London. University Press, Oxford.

Eaton, Gai (1994): *Islam and the Destiny of Man.* The Islamic Text Society, Cambridge.

Jay, C. (1995) *A Celebration of Life.* The Child Bereavement Charity (see 'Useful Addresses')

Kohner, N. & Henley, A. (1991) *When a Baby Dies.* Routledge, London and New York.

Sparshott, M.M. (1997) *Pain, Distress and the Newborn Baby.* Blackwell Science, Oxford.

Warden, A. (1999) *Benedict : A Child of Mine.* The Child Bereavement Charity, (see 'Useful Addresses')